The Samurai Sword

The
Samurai Sword

A HANDBOOK

by

John M. Yumoto

Charles E. Tuttle Company
Rutland, Vermont & Tokyo, Japan

Published by the Charles E. Tuttle Company, Inc.
of Rutland, Vermont & Tokyo, Japan
with editorial offices at Suido 1-chome, 2-6
Bunkyo-ku, Tokyo 112

Library of Congress Catalog
Card No. 58-7497

International Standard Book No. 0-8048-0509-1
First printing, 1958
Thirty-second printing, 1995

PRINTED IN SINGAPORE

Contents

List of Plates

List of Figures

Foreword

THE PURPOSE of this brief handbook is to furnish samurai-sword owners and collectors with information about their swords, to relate some of the intriguing history and legends surrounding them, and to emphasize their artistic value.

Because of the value of such swords, information about their proper care and maintenance is contained herein. It is hoped that some far-sighted individual will one day initiate a foundation whose sole purpose shall be to collect samurai swords and preserve their beauty for posterity as *objets d'art*.

Through the mist and fog of great antiquity, there remain the Three Sacred Treasures of Japan, which are still held in reverence by the people: the Sacred Mirror, the Comma-Shaped Beads, and the Sword—the three most highly prized national treasures in Japan. The fact that the Sword is listed among them is significant in that it indicates that the Japanese do not regard the sword as being merely a weapon. Some people collect these valuable and rare masterpieces as avidly as some seek old pistols and stamps.

In ancient times it was well established that anything suitable as an offering to the gods had to possess three elements: purity, rarity, and value. The sword was believed to have all of these characteristics, and it was a not uncommon practice to give one as a votive offering. According to records, the first such offering was made to the gods in 3 B.C. Later, the sword became the symbol of the samurai code and acquired further spiritual qualities.

The samurai code, or code of the warrior, is comparable to the code of honor of the European feudal period and was based primarily upon the mastery of arms, principally the sword. The samurai sword was a family heirloom, carefully preserved and passed on to each succeeding generation. Even in modern times these swords have been carried into battle by officers and men of the Japanese army and navy.

The swords collected by American soldiers in the recent war were regarded in many different lights. Most soldiers thought they were collecting only souvenirs, and seldom did they ever suspect the true value of the swords.

Immediately after the cessation of hostilities swords in Japan were confiscated by the Allies as weapons. Later, however, those having artistic or historical value were returned to their original owners to be preserved as *objets d'art*. The samurai sword remains in Japan and throughout the world as an impressive example of specialized workmanship culminating in fine art.

When the atomic bomb fell on Hiroshima, the samurai sword lost its prestige as a weapon, but it still remains the most perfect steel sword in the world. The Damascus and Toledo swords of folklore or the Excalibur blade of English literature could in no way compare with the workmanship and the quality of steel which went into the manufacture of the samurai sword.

John M. Yumoto

Acknowledgements

THE AUTHOR acknowledges his indebtedness to Mr. Randolph Bullock, Assistant Curator of Arms and Armor, Metropolitan Museum of Art, New York City; and Mr. Edwin G. Beal, Jr., Chief, Japanese Section, Library of Congress, Washington, D.C., for furnishing lists of English and Japanese publications on the subject.

For assistance in preparing the text and illustrations I am much indebted to my teachers and friends, in particular to Dr. Junji Homma, Mr. Kanichi Sato, and Mr. Susumu Kashima, of the Society for the Preservation of the Japanese Sword, National Museum, Tokyo, Japan; and Lieutenant Colonel George E. Slade, of the U.S. Army.

Gratitude is also due fellow members of the Northern California Sword Club.

They shall beat their swords into plowshares,...nation shall not lift up sword against nation, neither shall they learn war any more.

Isaiah II:4

The Samurai Sword

1

Japanese History and the Samurai Sword

THE HISTORY of the samurai sword is closely related to the history of Japan. For that reason this brief résumé of Japanese history is included.

THE PERIODS OF JAPANESE HISTORY

In considering the history of Japan and the samurai sword, it is convenient to have reference points. It is possible to divide Japanese history into the following periods:

1. ANCIENT PERIOD (before A.D. 650). Historians disagree as to the exact date, but about the same time as the beginning of the Christian Era, Jimmu, the first emperor of Japan, set out from Kyushu through the Inland Sea to Kashiwara, in Yamato Province (Fig. 1), and subjugated the hostile tribes, thereby establishing the Japanese Empire. Later, in about A.D. 284, continental culture, in the form of Confucian classics,

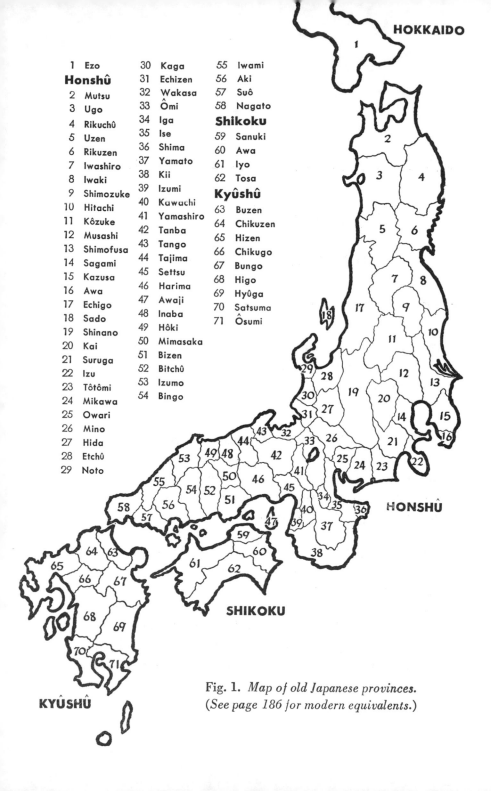

1	Ezo	30	Kaga	55	Iwami
Honshû		31	Echizen	56	Aki
2	Mutsu	32	Wakasa	57	Suô
3	Ugo	33	Ômi	58	Nagato
4	Rikuchû	34	Iga	**Shikoku**		
5	Uzen	35	Ise	59	Sanuki
6	Rikuzen	36	Shima	60	Awa
7	Iwashiro	37	Yamato	61	Iyo
8	Iwaki	38	Kii	62	Tosa
9	Shimozuke	39	Izumi	**Kyûshû**		
10	Hitachi	40	Kawachi	63	Buzen
11	Kôzuke	41	Yamashiro	64	Chikuzen
12	Musashi	42	Tanba	65	Hizen
13	Shimofusa	43	Tango	66	Chikugo
14	Sagami	44	Tajima	67	Bungo
15	Kazusa	45	Settsu	68	Higo
16	Awa	46	Harima	69	Hyûga
17	Echigo	47	Awaji	70	Satsuma
18	Sado	48	Inaba	71	Ôsumi
19	Shinano	49	Hôki		
20	Kai	50	Mimasaka		
21	Suruga	51	Bizen		
22	Izu	52	Bitchû		
23	Tôtômi	53	Izumo		
24	Mikawa	54	Bingo		
25	Owari				
26	Mino				
27	Hida				
28	Etchû				
29	Noto				

Fig. 1. *Map of old Japanese provinces.*
(See page 186 for modern equivalents.)

silk culture, and the art of weaponmaking, was introduced directly from China or Korea.

It is believed that there were many Chinese and Korean smiths who came to Japan and made swords. Even so, there are very few swords in existence that were made during this period in Japan or imported from the continent. Since the few extant swords from this period are similar in appearance, it is difficult to determine the locale of manufacture. Some have been unearthed from ancient tombs. They were not properly tempered, and the majority were of the straight type.

2. NARA PERIOD (650 to 793). At the beginning of this period a permanent capital was established at Nara, in Yamato Province. Prior to this time, there had been no permanent capital, the center of government being determined by the current ruling emperor. Buddhism flourished, and this period is known as the "Golden Age" of religious art, architecture, painting, and sculpture. The Taika Reform (645), which marked the beginning of the Nara period, again established the imperial family as the absolute rulers of Japan, and new national laws were introduced. The art of swordmaking was still primitive and made but little progress. However, in order to equip the national army, there arose a great demand for a better sword.

3. HEIAN PERIOD (794 to 1191). The capital was moved from Nara to Heian, or present-day Kyoto, in Yamashiro Province; and power of administration was shifted from the royal family to the Fujiwara clan, who had managed to marry their daughters into the royal family and thus had obtained control of the government. During a period of eight reigns, a total of one hundred years, the Fujiwara clan ruled as regents, and

there was relative peace in the land. But the extravagance of the Fujiwaras and their costly administration of the government placed an increasing burden on the peasantry and caused them to desert their farms and crafts and become lawless highwaymen. About the year 900, taking advantage of this situation, the two samurai clans of Minamoto and Taira came to power and replaced the Fujiwaras.

The urge for contact with China died down, perhaps because the Japanese no longer felt inferior to the Chinese. Instead, they devoted themselves, in their own way, to the improvement of their once-imported culture. The art of swordmaking made tremendous progress during this period, and Japanese smiths began to produce better and better swords. Samurai swordmaking reached its zenith during the latter half of this period.

4. KAMAKURA PERIOD (1192 to 1336). Establishment of the shogunate, or feudal government, at Kamakura, in Sagami (Soshu) Province, by the Minamoto clan marked the beginning of the Kamakura period and 675 years of feudalism under shogunate military supreme command, which had both administrative and judicial power. In 1274 and 1281 the Mongols, in the backwash of their invasion of Europe, attempted to invade Japan. However, they were defeated by warriors from Kamakura with the help of two sudden typhoons, which the Japanese believed were sent by the gods.

These national emergencies demanded new and stronger types of swords. The school of smiths in Sagami Province perfected swords which have never been surpassed.

Following the invasions and as luxury was introduced into the formerly simple samurai life, the power of the shogunate declined. Finally, the Emperor Godaigo, with the aid of the

Ashikaga clan, succeeded in overthrowing the shogunate capital and regaining control of the government.

5. MUROMACHI (ASHIKAGA) PERIOD (1337 to 1573). The Ashikaga clan betrayed the Emperor Godaigo, set up its own puppet government at Kyoto, and re-established the shogunate system. However, Godaigo escaped from the Ashikagas to the Hill of Yoshino, near Nara. For fifty-five years (1337 to 1392) there were two imperial courts in Japan. This was a dark period in Japanese history. Because the Ashikagas were never very strong, they were unable to control the provinces, and there was constant fighting between the feudal lords. This period of wars (the Sengoku period) lasted over a hundred years (1467 to 1574). The demand for swords increased, and smiths made them in great numbers throughout Japan. In Kyoto the arts flourished under the extravagant patronage of the Ashikaga shoguns, who imitated the Fujiwaras, even surpassing them in splendor and luxury.

6. AZUCHI-MOMOYAMA PERIOD (1574 to 1602). Oda Nobunaga, a samurai of low birth, came to Kyoto at the request of the emperor to restore order, and was appointed vice-shogun. Before completing his task of unifying Japan, Nobunaga was assassinated. Toyotomi Hideyoshi, Nobunaga's able lieutenant, completed the task of unification and restoring order in Japan after the long period of wars. Hideyoshi, of humble birth, was appointed regent of the empire, and all other military leaders became self-appointed daimyos, or feudal lords. Peace brought to Hideyoshi the problem of the disposition of a huge, now-unnecessary army. To put this army to use, Hideyoshi made two unsuccessful invasions of Korea and China, first

in 1592 and again in 1597. During this period, Hideyoshi made his capital in Osaka. All arts, including the making of swords and mountings, flourished.

7. EDO (TOKUGAWA) PERIOD (1603 to 1867). After Hideyoshi's death and following the battle of Sekigahara (September 1600), power shifted from the Toyotomi clan to Tokugawa Ieyasu. The Tokugawa clan ruled all of Japan from their capital in Edo, or present-day Tokyo, for more than 250 years. At the beginning of this period, the Tokugawas, in order to perpetuate the shogunate system and make it capable of functioning smoothly under ordinary leadership, established fundamental laws for the shoguns, the nobles, and the samurais. They also adopted a closed-door policy toward foreign countries. A unique and rigid class system, which divided the people into daimyo, samurai, farmer, artisan, and merchant, was established and carried on during this period. The long and relatively peaceful Tokugawa period came to an end in the early nineteenth century, when foreign powers attempted to open Japan to outside commerce. It was at this time that the Sotozama daimyos, the descendants of the lords who had made peace with Tokugawa after the battle of Sekigahara, arose in opposition to the shogunate.

8. MODERN PERIOD (since 1868). Emperor Meiji, the 122nd descendant of Emperor Jimmu, aided by the Sotozama daimyos, regained sovereignty from the Tokugawa clan and moved the capital to Tokyo in 1868. Shortly thereafter (1876) wearing of the sword was prohibited by national decree.

Legend has it that the swordsmith Amakuni made the first

samurai sword in Yamato about A.D. 700. Although there is no historical proof of this, the legend seems logical, since some of the earliest swords found today can be traced back to the swordsmith Yasutsuna, of Hoki, and date from about 900. Amakuni was the head of a group of swordsmiths who were all employed at that time in making swords for the emperor and his warriors (Fig. 2).

One day Amakuni and his son, Amakura, were standing in the doorway of their shop, watching the soldiers as they returned from battle. The emperor then passed by but did not give Amakuni any sign of recognition as he had done on previous occasions. Amakuni had always looked upon these gestures as a sign of appreciation for his efforts. Then he

Fig. 2.   *Swordsmiths at work.*

suddenly noticed that nearly half of the returning soldiers were carrying broken swords.

Amakuni and his son went about gathering the sword remnants and examining them. It appeared to him that the chief reasons for the breakages were that the swords had been improperly forged and that the soldiers had hit hard objects with them. As he remembered the emperor's subtle rebuff, his eyes filled with tears and he muttered to himself, "If they are going to use our swords for such slashing, I shall make one which will not break."

Taking this vow, Amakuni and his son shut themselves away in the forge and prayed for seven days and seven nights to the Shinto gods. Then Amakuni selected the best sand ore he could obtain and refined it. Steadily, relentlessly, the two worked at their apparently impossible task. Thirty days later, gaunt, weary, but jubilant, the swordsmiths emerged with a single-bladed sword which had curvature. The other sword-smiths believed them to be insane, but they ground and polished the new sword.

In the months that followed, Amakuni and his son continued with their work, turning out many improved types of swords. In the following spring there was another war. Again the soldiers returned, and as he watched them pass by he counted: one, two, three—twenty-five, twenty-six, twenty-seven—thirty, thirty-one. All the swords were coming back from the front intact and perfect! As the emperor passed him, he smiled and said, "You are an expert swordmaker. None of the swords you made failed in this battle." Amakuni rejoiced and once more felt that all was right and his life was full. (This legend comes from the smiths of Yamato Province.)

PERIODS IN THE HISTORY OF THE SAMURAI SWORD

In general, weapons which come under the category of samurai swords are: (1) made of steel; (2) single bladed; (3) curved; (4) tempered. The history of such swords is usually divided into the following four periods:

1. ANCIENT SWORD (CHOKUTO OR KEN) PERIOD (until A.D. 900). These swords were made chiefly by smiths from China or Korea or by the early Japanese smiths. Although they were made of steel, the tempering was faulty. They were mostly of the straight *(chokuto)* type. The centers of the swordmaking profession were in Yamato, Mutsu, and San-in. Although these swords were made in Japan, they were mere imitations of Chinese blades. High-ranking officers usually carried expensive swords made in China (Fig. 3). This imitation of the Chinese sword was gradually developed into the typical samurai sword.

Fig. 3. *An official of the mid-Heian period (800–900) with a lightly curved sword.*

2. OLD SWORD (KOTO) PERIOD (900 to 1530). With the disintegration of the peaceful civil administration under the Fujiwara clan in the latter half of the Heian period, there arose the new samurai class. Power was obtained only by means of

Fig. 4. *Warriors of the Old Sword period.*

warfare. Since wars for power were numerous, the samurai adopted the sword for combat. The leaders made full use of their warriors on horseback at the battle fronts (Fig. 4). Thus, swords which had a cutting edge of four feet or more were often employed.

The predominant weapons used were bows and arrows, *naginata* (a kind of halberd), and swords. The sword became an everyday weapon and was carried constantly. The straight sword which was employed prior to this period, principally for stabbing, was replaced by a single-bladed sword with curvature. The transition from the old straight style into the standard samurai-sword style, however, took a long time. There are few swords which were made during the transitory period still in existence today.

About the year 900 a smith in Hoki by the name of Yasu-tsuna began forging excellent samurai swords. There has been very little change in style since then.

By tempering steel from iron ore or iron sand, the sword-smiths succeeded in fashioning nearly perfect swords with their primitive tools. The most famous swordsmiths appear in Japanese history between the years 900 to 1450.

To a large extent the location of the smiths was governed by the following factors: proximity to the center of administration, where the demand for swords was usually great; easy access to ore and charcoal used for forging; a plentiful supply of good water; a mild climate.

Schools of smiths from five provinces, Bizen, Yamashiro, Yamato, Soshu, and Mino, produced approximately eighty per cent of all swords made in this period. Collectively these smiths were known as the Five Schools. There were several branches of each school, and each province developed and maintained its own traditional and distinctive methods of swordmaking.

a. The Bizen School. The province of Bizen consisted of the southern half of present-day Okayama Prefecture. Since Bizen was close to the continent, it is believed that the art of swordmaking was introduced there at a very early date. Conditions there were ideal for swordmaking, and for a thousand years the village of Osafune, in the eastern section of the province, was a center of that activity.

It is believed that Tomonari (c. 1100) was the founder of the Bizen School. He was followed by Kanehira, Sukehira, Nobufusa, Takahira, and Masatsune. These smiths are known as the Early Bizen *(Ko-Bizen)* School.

The following are the several branches of the Bizen School and their leading smiths:

1) Fukuoka Branch (Kamakura period): Norimune, Sukemune, Muneyoshi, Yoshifusa, Norifusa, Naganori.

2) Yoshioka Branch (Kamakura period): Sukeyoshi, Sukemitsu.

3) Osafune Branch (Kamakura period): Mitsutada, Kage-
hide, Nagamitsu, Kagemitsu, Sanenaga, Chikakage, Ka-
nemitsu, Norimitsu, Motomitsu, Nagayoshi, Nagashige,
Motoshige, Shigezane; (Ashikaga period): Moromitsu,
Yasumitsu, Morimitsu, Sukemitsu, Sukesada, Katsumitsu,
Tadamitsu, Kiyomitsu.

4) Yoshii Branch (Kamakura period): Kagenori; (Ashikaga period): Naganori, Kiyonori.

5) Omiya Branch (Kamakura period): Morokage, Morikage; (Ashikaga period): Morikage, Morokage.

b. The Yamashiro School. Kyoto, the center of Yamashiro
Province, was the imperial capital from 794 until 1868. Here
the sword was in great demand. Munechika (c. 987) was a
forerunner of this school. The branches of the Yamashiro
School and their leading smiths are:

1) Sanjo Branch (Heian period): Munechika, Yoshiie,
Kanenaga, Kuninaga; (Ashikaga period): Yoshinori.

2) Awataguchi Branch (Kamakura period): Hisakuni,
Kuniyasu, Kunitsuna, Norikuni, Kuniyoshi, Yoshimitsu.

3) Rai Branch (Kamakura period): Kuniyuki, Kunitoshi,
Ryokai, Mitsukane, Kunimitsu, Kunitsugu.

4) Ayakoji Branch (Kamakura period): Sadatoshi, Sadayoshi, Sadatsugu.

5) Nobukuni Branch (Ashikaga period): Nobukuni, Nobu-
sada.

6) Hasebe Branch (Ashikaga period): Kunishige, Kuni-
nobu.

7) Heian-jo Branch (Ashikaga period): Nagayoshi.

c. The Yamato School. It is believed that there were many good smiths around Nara, in Yamato Province, when Nara was the capital. However, the majority of them moved to Kyoto in 794, when Kyoto became the capital. About 1200, smiths again gathered at Nara, when various religious sects which had begun to rise to power in the city needed arms for their monks. Names of temples were mainly used for branches of this school:

1) Toma Branch (Kamakura period): Kuniyuki, Aritoshi.
2) Tegai Branch (Kamakura period): Kanenaga; (Ashikaga period): Kanenage, Kaneuji, Kanezane, Kaneyoshi, Kanetoshi.
3) Hosho Branch (Kamakura period): Sadatsugu, Sadamune, Sadayoshi.
4) Shirikage Branch (Kamakura period): Norinaga; (Ashikaga period): Norinaga.
5) Senju-in Branch (Kamakura period): Yasushige, Yoshihiro.

d. The Soshu (Sagami) School. The center of swordmaking in this province was the town of Kamakura, where Minamoto Yoritomo, the first shogun, established his shogunate government in 1192. Although conditions in Kamakura were not favorable for this art, Kamakura attracted many skillful smiths from all over the nation because of its intensely military atmosphere. The branches and their outstanding smiths were:

1) Yamashiro Branch (composed of smiths who came from Yamashiro and who flourished during the Kamakura

period): Kunitsuna, Kunimitsu, Kunihiro, Kuniyasu.

2) Bizen Branch (composed of smiths who came from Bizen: Kamakura period): Kunimune, Sukezane.

3) Soshu Branch (Kamakura period): Yukimitsu, Masamune; (Ashikaga period): Sadamune, Hiromitsu, Akihiro, Masahiro, Hiromasa, Tsunahiro, Yasukuni.

e. The Mino School. The center of the Mino School was the town of Seki, near Gifu, and for this reason this school is also known as the Seki School. It is believed that it was established by students of Masamune, of Soshu. Early works of this school are very good and are difficult to distinguish from those of Soshu. However, the majority of the swords made shortly thereafter and also during the later part of the period were poor. Branches and leading smiths of this school were:

1) Kaneuji Branch (Kamakura period): Kaneuji; (Ashikaga period): Kaneuji, Kanetomo, Kanetsugu, Kanemitsu, Kanetsune, Kanefusa, Kaneyoshi, Kanesada, Kanemoto.

2) Kaneshige (Kinju) Branch (Ashikaga period): Kaneshige (Kinju), Kaneyuki.

In the Old Sword period the art of swordmaking also flourished in other provinces of Japan. During the Heian period outstanding smiths were: Yasutsuna; Sanemori; Aritsuna; Nichijo, in Hoki; Moritsugu, in Bitchu; Joshu (Sadahide), in Bungo; and Yukiyasu, in Satsuma. The following list shows some of the leading smiths of the Kamakura period:

Bitchû Province	Sadatsugu, Tsunetsugu, Kanetsugu, Masatsune, Suketsugu, Shigetsugu, Yoshitsugu, Tsuguyoshi, Hidetsugu, Norifusa, Sanetoshi
Bingo Province	Masaie
Suô Province	Kiyotsuna
Chikuzen Province	Sairen, Jitsua, Sa
Chikugo Province	Mitsuyo
Bungo Province	Yukihira
Higo Province	Kunimura, Kunitomo, Kuniyoshi, Kunitoki, Kunisuke
Mutsu Province	Hôju
Etchû Province	Yoshihiro, Norishige

The following are smiths of the early Ashikaga (Yoshino) period:

Settsu Province	Kuninaga
Ômi Province	Sadamune, Toshinaga
Echizen Province	Nagayoshi
Etchû Province	Tametsugu
Kaga Province	Sanekage
Iwami Province	Naotsuna, Sadatsuna
Bitchû Province	Sadatsugu, Tsugiyoshi, Tsuginao
Bingo Province	Masahiro, Masanobu, Masakiyo, Ichijô, Kaneyasu
Suô Province	Kiyotsuna
Nagato Province	Yasuyoshi, Moriyoshi
Chikuzen Province	Yasuyoshi, Yoshisada, Kunihiro
Bungo Province	Tomoyuki, Toshiyuki
Hizen Province	Kunitoki, Kuniyoshi

The following are smiths of the late Ashikaga period:

Ise Province	Muramasa, Masashige
Suruga Province	Gisuke, Sukemune, Hirosuke
Mutsu Province	Hôju, Morimune
Uzen Province	Gasan

Wakasa Province	Munenaga, Muneyoshi, Fuyuhiro
Etchû Province	Kunifusa, Kunimune, Kunitsugu
Echigo Province	Nagayoshi, Masanobu
Kaga Province	Tomoshige, Yukimitsu, Nobunaga, Kiyomitsu, Kagemitsu, Ietsugu
Inaba Province	Kagenaga, Yukikage
Iwami Province	Tadatsuna
Bitchû Province	Kunishige, Nagatsugu, Kagetsugu
Bingo Province	Masaie, Masahiro, Masanobu, Ichijô, Kanemori, Mitsushige
Suô Province	Kiyotsuna, Kiyosada
Nagato Province	Akikuni, Yukikuni
Chikuzen Province	Moritaka
Chikugo Province	Ienaga, Norinaga
Buzen Province	Yoshizane, Yoshisada
Bungo Province	Yoshizane, Yoshikane, Nagamori, Shigenori
Higo Province	Masakuni
Hizen Province	Kuniyoshi, Kunitoki
Satsuma Province	Yasuyuki
Kii Province	Sanetsuna, Sanetsugu
Sanuki Province	Ujiyoshi, Yasuyoshi
Tosa Province	Yoshimitsu

The seventy years following 1467 are known as the Sengoku period and were marked by a series of feudal civil wars. To meet the increasing need for swords, the smiths turned out blades in mass production. Because of the methods employed and because the swordsmiths no longer refined their own steel, swords of an inferior quality resulted. Today, despite the large number of swords from the Sengoku period still in existence, relatively few can be considered very good.

In the middle of the sixteenth century, the merit of swordsmiths won official recognition from the emperor. He bestowed

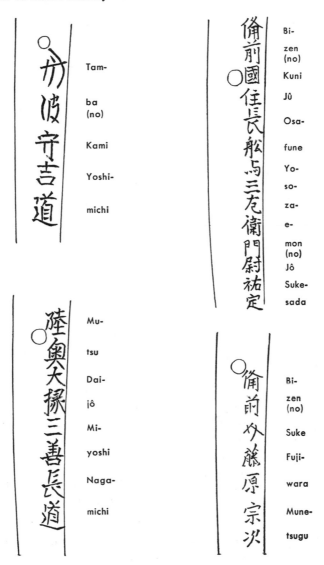

Tam-
ba
(no)
Kami
Yoshi-
michi

Bi-
zen
(no)
Kuni
Jô
Osa-
fune
Yo-
so-
za-
e-
mon
(no)
Jô
Suke-
sada

Mu-
tsu
Dai-
jô
Mi-
yoshi
Naga-
michi

Bi-
zen
(no)
Suke
Fuji-
wara
Mune-
tsugu

Fig. 5.   *Inscribed titles on tangs.   (Miyoshi is also read Sanzen.)*

titles on certain smiths, and usually the name of a province and the title was prefixed to the smith's first name. *Suke, Jo, Daijo,* and *Kami* were the titles most frequently bestowed (Fig. 5).

3. NEW SWORD (SHINTO) PERIOD (1530 to 1867). Oda Nobunaga and Toyotomi Hideyoshi brought the long civil wars to an end. This war period was replaced by a peaceful interim, in which the sword lost its functional value. In addition, the length of the long sword *(daito)* was shortened, the cutting edge being reduced to about two feet, and the samurai began carrying it by inserting it between the hip and the sash (Fig. 6).

During the early part of the New Sword period, when the Osaka-Kyoto area was the center of administration, there were many skilled swordsmiths in that region. The traditional and distinctive methods of the Five Schools were lost, and nearly all castle towns became centers of the swordmaking art.

Fig. 6. *Formally attired samurai of the Edo period with two swords in his sash.*

In the Tokugawa period, Edo (Tokyo) was the center of swordmaking and attracted many good smiths, but toward the end of the period, the art of swordmaking declined and emphasis was placed more upon looks than usefulness. The smiths were placing "gingerbread" on their products, and one can find on the swords of this period extravagant engravings of flowers, shrubbery, and dragons, instead of the simple Sanskrit characters or grooves of older swords. Even in the tempered lines of the swords there may be found intricate and picturesque representations of maple leaves, cherry blossoms, chrysanthemums, and Mount Fuji. More than half of the samurai swords in existence today were made during the New Sword period.

The following list shows some of the leading smiths of the early (Azuchi-Momoyama) part of this period. Titles or surnames are enclosed in parentheses:

Yamashiro Province	(Umetada) Myôju, (Shinano no Kami) Kunihiro, Kuniyasu, (Deba Daijô) Kunimichi, (Echigo no Kami) Kunitomo, (Ôsumi no Jô) Masahiro, (Iga no Kami) Kanamichi, (Tamba no Kami) Yoshimichi, (Etchû no Kami) Masatoshi, (Izumi no Kami) Kunisada, (Kôchi no Kami) Kunisuke
Settsu Province	(Izumi no Kami) Kunisada, (Kôchi no Kami) Kunisuke, (Soboro) Sukehiro, (Tamba no Kami) Yoshimichi, (Omi no Kami) Tadatsuna, (Mutsu no Kami) Kanemori
Mino Province	(Sagami no Kami) Masatsune, (Mino no Kami) Masatsune, (Hôki no Kami) Nobutaka, (Hidachi no Kami) Ujifusa
Musashi Province	Hankei, Yasutsugu, (Musashi Daijô) Korekazu
Ômi Province	Ippô
Iwashiro Province	Nagakuni, (Mutsu Daijô) Nagamichi
Rikuzen Province	(Yamashiro Daijô) Kunikane, (Yamato Daijô) Yasusada

Wakasa Province	(Wakasa no Kami) Fuyuhiro
Echizen Province	(Higo Daijô) Sadakuni, Yasutsugu, (Yamato Daijô) Masanori
Kaga Province	Kanewaka, Takahira, Katsukuni
Bitchû Province	(Ôyogo) Kunishige
Aki Province	(Higo no Kami) Teruhiro, (Harima no Kami) Teruhiro
Kii Province	Shigekuni
Bizen Province	Sukesada
Hizen Province	Tadayoshi, (Ômi Daijô) Masahiro, (Kawachi Daijô) Masahiro, (Deba no Kami) Yukihiro
Satsuma Province	(Izu no Kami) Masafusa

The following is a list of leading smiths of the Edo period, or latter part of the New Sword period.

Yamashiro Province	Yoshinobu, Yoshihira, (Iga no Kami) Kanamichi, (Tamba no Kami) Yoshimichi, (Ômi no Kami) Hisamichi
Settsu Province	Shinkai, Harukuni, (Echizen no Kami) Sukehiro, (Ômi no Kami) Sukenao, (Kawachi no Kami) Kunisuke, (Higo no Kami) Kuniyasu, (Ise no Kami) Kuniteru, (Yamato no Kami) Yoshimichi, (Ikkanshi) Tadatsuna, Nagatsuna, (Tatara) Chôkô, (Echigo no Kami) Kanesada, Terukane
Musashi Province	Kotetsu, Okimasa, Okinao, Yasutsugu, (Ômi no Kami) Tsuguhira, (Musashi Daijô) Korekazu, (Tsushima no Kami) Tsunemitsu, Mitsuhira, (Ômi no Kami) Masahiro, (Tajima no Kami) Sadakuni, (Suishinshi) Masahide, (Chikuzen Daijô) Naotane, Naokatsu, Kiyomaro, (Chikuzen no Kami) Nobuhide, Masao, (Sa) Yukihide

Hidachi Province	Kaboku, Bokuden
Rikuzen Province	(Yamashiro no Kami) Kunikane, Yasutomo
Bizen Province	Sukesada, Sukenaga, Kunimune
Satsuma Province	(Hôki no Kami) Masayoshi, (Yamato no Kami) Motohira

4. MODERN SWORD (SHIN-SHINTO) PERIOD (after 1868). Emperor Meiji ascended the throne just three years after the start of this period and introduced the Meiji Restoration, which caused Japan to modernize and begin to keep pace with the rest of the world—truly the greatest single event in Japanese history. The feudal system came to an end, and with it, the prestige of the samurai. Swords could no longer be worn. The swordsmiths thereby lost their trade and turned to ordinary blacksmithing. They made hoes, scissors, knives, horseshoes, and the like, for their livelihood. Since that time and up to the present, there has not been a single great swordsmith. In the Meiji era (1868 to 1912) swords, guards, and handle ornaments were exported, chiefly to France and the United States. The turn of the century was the zenith of sword collectors in the United States, and many books concerning swords and sword ornaments were published at that time. Museum exhibits of swords and sword mountings in the present day are composed of items from these collections.

In the beginning of the Showa era (1926 to present) nationalistic ideas gained power. Swordmaking, even though on a small scale, was revived to a considerable extent so that at the annual Imperial Academy Art Exhibition a sword section was opened. Shortly before the beginning of World War II there were about one hundred craftsmen in Japan who made swords as a side line.

Many blades made by smiths of the Showa era have a stamping of a cherry blossom with the character for *Sho* of Showa above the signature of the smith on the tang. (Figs. 7 and 8).

Fig. 7. *Stamp found on many blades of the Showa era. Cherry-blossom design with character for* Sho. (*Actual diameter* 1/8".)

Many swords, such as police sabers, parade sabers, and the like, which were manufactured during the last forty or fifty years cannot be considered samurai swords because of plating or chemical treatment and methods of forging contrary to the conventional methods of hand-forging and tempering of samurai swords.

Fig. 8. *Tang rubbing of a blade made in the Showa era by Shoshinshi Fukumoto Kumemune. Note cherry-blossom emblem with the character for* Sho *above the signature.*

STATISTICS ON SWORDSMITHS AND SWORDS

According to available records, there was a total of about thirteen thousand swordsmiths throughout Japanese history until the Meiji Restoration, in 1868. If the number of those who made swords as a hobby and the smiths of unauthenticated existence were to be included, the total would be approximately twenty thousand. Assuming that each swordsmith averaged one

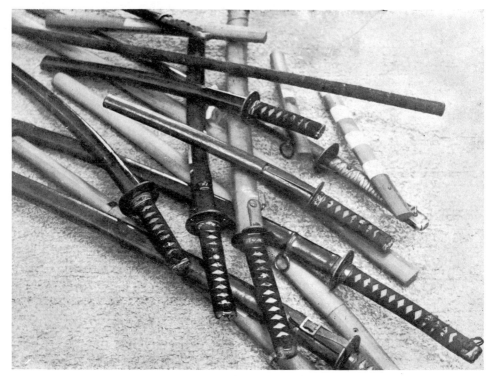

Plate 1. *A collection of swords brought back to the U.S. by a serviceman.*

Plate 2.   Daito (*long sword*).

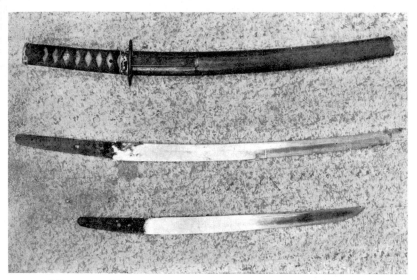

Plate 3. *Top:* wakizashi (*medium sword*) *in* buke-zukuri *mounting.* *Middle:* wakizashi *blade of* shino-zukuri *type* (*i.e., with ridge line*). *Bottom:* wakizashi *blade of* hira-zukuri *type* (*i.e., without ridge line*).

Plate 4. Tanto (*short sword*) *in a silver mounting.* *A handle which is not bound with tapes, such as is illustrated here, is often employed with a ceremonial* jindachi-zukuri *mounting.*

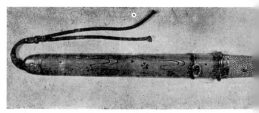

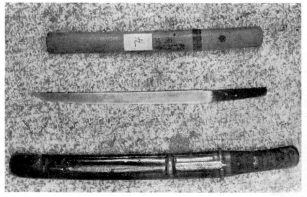

Plate 5. *Top:* tanto *in* shirasaya *mounting.* *The inscriptions are the collector's reference notes.* *Middle:* tanto *blade of* hirazukuri *type.* *Bottom:* tanto *in* buke-zukuri *mounting.*

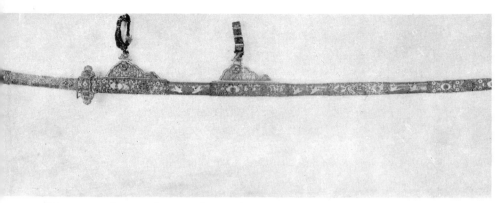

Plate 6. *A straight sword in a* ken *mounting.*

Plate 7. *A long sword in a* jindachi-zukuri *mounting.*
Note that the handle is not bound with tapes.

Plate 8. *A long sword in a* jindachi-zukuri *mounting.*
Note the tape bindings.

Plate 9. *Painting depicting a samurai of the mid-Edo period. The air of swords in his sash are in* buke-zukuri *mountings.*

hundred swords, a not unreasonable estimate, the total number of samurai swords can be placed at about two million.

Prior to World War II there were approximately one-and-a-half million swords (including factory-made ones) in existence, nearly one-third of which were over two feet in length *(daito)*. About two hundred thousand of this number were made by the Japanese government in sword factories and by smiths after the Meiji Restoration. At present, there are no more than one hundred thousand swords in Japan. In fact, there are more samurai swords in the United States today than there are in Japan. An estimated 250,000 to 350,000 swords have been brought into this country as war souvenirs by returning servicemen (Plate 1). Most of these are long swords *(daito)*, formerly used by Japanese commissioned and non-commissioned officers. About seventy per cent of the long swords in existence today are in the United States. Swords of the *buke-zukuri* type constitute the bulk of those brought back to the United States by returning servicemen. Second in number are swords of the neo-army *(shin-gunto)* type, followed by those of the proto-army *(kyu-gunto)* type, police sabers, army parade sabers, and navy types. Very few of the *ken* and *jindachi-zukuri* types have been brought into the United States.

2

Types of Swords

SAMURAI SWORDS may be classified by length or by the type of mounting in which they are found.

CLASSIFICATION OF SWORDS BY LENGTH

Three types of samurai swords can be differentiated by the length measurement of their cutting edges. For measuring swords (and most other objects) the Japanese use the *shaku* and its fractions as their standard:

$$10 \; rin = 1 \; bu \quad = 0.119305 \text{ inch}$$
$$10 \; bu \; = 1 \; sun \quad = 1.193054 \text{ inches}$$
$$10 \; sun = 1 \; shaku = 11.930542 \text{ inches}$$

1. LONG SWORD (DAITO): over two *shaku* in length. These are the longer of the two swords commonly worn by the samurai. There are many good swords of this length. It is very difficult

to temper a *daito* evenly from tip to base because of its great length (Plate 2).

2. MEDIUM SWORD (WAKIZASHI): between one and two *shaku* in length. These were worn by samurai as auxiliary swords, or by persons of non-samurai classes, who were allowed to wear no more than one sword of a length no longer than two *shaku*. Good swords in this length are scarce (Plate 3).

3. SHORT SWORD (TANTO): less than one *shaku* in length. These, the shorter of the two swords worn by the samurai, served as auxiliary weapons. Also, women and tradesmen used them as protective weapons. Usually they are of the *hira-zukuri* (without ridge line) type. They are commonly, though vulgarly, called hara-kiri knives (Plates 4 and 5).

CLASSIFICATION OF SWORDS BY MOUNTINGS

Regardless of their length, swords can be differentiated by their mountings into six classes.

1. KEN MOUNTINGS. These straight mountings are the oldest type known, being for swords of the Ancient Sword period (before 900). There are few still in existence. Of the swords found in these mountings, some were made with single-edged and some with double-edged blades (Plate 6).

2. JINDACHI-ZUKURI MOUNTINGS. Mountings of this type were for the long sword of the Old Sword (Koto) period (900 to 1530) and were four to five feet in length. In this period the sword was worn suspended from the hip by cords which passed

through two rings on the scabbard (Plates 7 and 8). There are many imitations of the *jindachi-zukuri* mounting. Most of them were copied in the past one hundred years in the vicinity of Tokyo, Kyoto, Nara, and Sakai (near Osaka), where much counterfeiting was done not only of mountings but of well-known blades.

3. BUKE-ZUKURI MOUNTINGS. These mountings come from the New Sword (Shinto) period (1531 to 1867). The handle is bound with narrow tape or leather thongs. Because the swords were worn on the left hip, inserted between the hip and the sash and not suspended, there were no rings attached to the scabbards, as in the *jindachi-zukuri* mountings. The full length of this mounting was three-and-a-half to four-and-a-half feet (Plates 9 and 10). Of all the mountings in existence, this type is most common and is of great interest to connoisseurs. The scabbard of the *buke-zukuri* mounting often has pockets for a *kozuka* (utility knife), a *kogai* (skewer), or a set of *wari-bashi* (split chopsticks) near its mouth (Plate 11). At first the *kozuka* was used as a dirk; in time, however, it came to be used as a utility knife. The blade section of the *kozuka* was usually made by a swordsmith and was of the *kata-kiri-ba* type (ridge line on only one side of the blade). The *kozuka* is polished only on the flat side. The handle section of the *kozuka* was made by the same artisan who made the ornaments, such as pommels *(fuchi* and *kashira)*, hilt ornaments *(menuki)*, guards *(tsuba)*, and the like. The *kogai* was used as a bodkin for the samurai's hair-do. It was commonly carried in a pocket in the scabbard of a *wakizashi* (medium-length sword). A projecting section at the base of the handle was used as an ear cleaner. It has a dull edge and is now frequently used as a letter opener. The

shape of the two *wari-bashi* together is similar to that of the *kogai*. Usually the *kogai* or *wari-bashi* were made by the same artisan who made the base of the *kozuka*. At the most, only two of these three items were carried in the pockets of a scabbard.

4. SHIRA-SAYA MOUNTINGS. These mountings were made of plain wood and were used in place of the original mounting to protect the blade or to replace a damaged mounting. This type has no guard. *Shira-saya* mountings were frequently made by the artisans following the Meiji Restoration: they lacked the skill to produce more elaborate mountings. This type is also called *yasume-zaya* (resting scabbard) and is convenient for protecting a blade or an original mounting. When a blade is not kept in its original mounting, a substitue blade *(tsunagi)* of wood or bamboo is inserted to preserve the mounting (Plate 12).

5. GUNTO (ARMY AND NAVY SWORDS) AND THEIR MOUNTINGS. After the Meiji Restoration the samurai class gave way to His Imperial Majesty's army and navy. The members of the army and navy carried regulation sabers of Western style made at modern government factories. However, in wartime most of them carried samurai swords in regular military mountings.

a. Kyu-gunto (proto-army sword) mountings. The scabbard of the proto-army type was chrome plated. The handle was wrapped with shark or giant-ray skin, which, in turn, was bound with gold-colored wire. The hand guard was a strip of metal starting at the base of the hilt, curving upward over the hand, and ending at the top of the hilt, somewhat in the manner of an English naval cutlass (Plate 13). Most of the officers who engaged in the Sino-Japanese war (1895 to 1896) and the Russo-Japanese war (1905 to 1906) used samurai swords in *buke-zukuri* mountings. However, some of the commissioned and non-commissioned officers used samurai swords in the regular military mountings.

The Japanese police have also used sabers generally similar to the above but narrower. The sword blades were made of plated steel, which gave the impression of a tempered edge. The plated edge, however, differs from the hand-tempered edge in that it has a very narrow blade with a perfect symmetrical wavy pattern. These swords have absolutely no value. Similar sabers were used by Japanese army officers during peacetime for parade purposes (Plate 14).

b. Shin-gunto (neo-army sword) mountings. In 1937 the Japanese military began to use a new type of regulation mounting called *shin-gunto.* The scabbard of this type resembles that of the *jindachi-zukuri* mounting but is made of brown-colored metal; however, this was usually covered with leather when used in a combat area (Plate 15). The handle resembles that of the *buke-zukuri* type in that it is bound by leather thongs or cord. The handle usually has cherry-blossom designs on its pommels and ornaments. This type always has a colored tassel to distinguish officer ranks: blue, for company grade; red, for field grade; red and gold, for general grade.

In the Showa era many blades of this type were turned out by government shops or by unskilled smiths between 1937 and 1945 and have little or no value.

Another type quite similar to the above was chiefly used by noncommissioned officers. The handle was made of cast iron, but since it was colored brown, it had the appearance of being leather or cord bound (Plate 16). These blades were made by government factories and can generally be identified by arabic numerals in the ridge area. The blade usually has an indistinct ridge line, resulting from machine polishing.

c. Kaigunto (naval sword) mountings. Swords used by the officers of the Japanese navy are of three types (Plate 17). One is represented by a short sword about fifteen inches long. The second type is long and bears a close resemblance to the *jindachi-zukuri* type or neo-army type, having two rings attached to its dark-blue scabbard. Some officers used old samurai swords in the mountings of the first and second types. The third type is also long, but narrow, and looks much like a police saber. Nearly all of the blades of the first and third types were factory made and have absolutely no value.

6. SHIKOMI-ZUE (SWORD CANE) MOUNTINGS. Almost all of the mountings of this type were made after the Meiji Restoration. The majority of blades in this mounting are of a poor grade (Plate 18).

3

Parts of the Sword

THE SWORD is composed of two main parts: the blade, and
the mountings.

THE BLADE

The composite parts of the blade are classified as follows
(Fig. 9):

1. THE POINT (KISSAKI). The point is the most difficult part
of a sword to forge and polish. The value of a sword is greatly
determined by the condition of its point. Tempered lines *(boshi)*
on a point need not necessarily be identical on both sides of
the blade.

a. Points can be classified, regardless of size, into two types
(Fig. 10):
  1) Straight-edge point *(fukura-kareru).*
  2) Curved-edge point *(fukura-tsuku).*

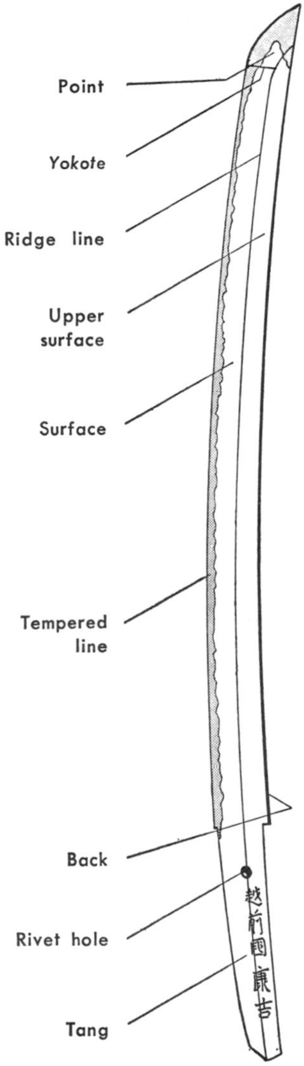

Point

Yokote

Ridge line

Upper
surface

Surface

Tempered
line

Back

Rivet hole

Tang

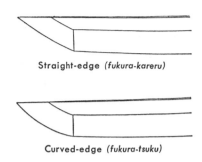

Straight-edge *(fukura-kareru)*

Curved-edge *(fukura-tsuku)*

Fig. 10. *Points classified by shape.*

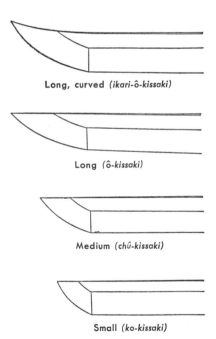

Long, curved *(ikari-ô-kissaki)*

Long *(ô-kissaki)*

Medium *(chû-kissaki)*

Small *(ko-kissaki)*

Fig. 9. *Parts of the blade*
(shinogi-zukuri *type*).

Fig. 11. *Points classified by size
and shape.*

b. Points can be classified by size and shape into four types (Fig. 11):

   1) Small point *(ko-kissaki)*.
   2) Medium point *(chu-kissaki)*.
   3) Long point *(o-kissaki)*.
   4) Long, curved point *(ikari-o-kissaki)*.

c. Points can be classified by their tempered lines *(boshi)* into ten types (Fig. 12):

   1) Large circle *(o-maru)*.
   2) Small circle *(ko-maru)*.
   3) Head shape *(jizo)*.
   4) No turn-back *(yaki-zume)*. Tempered patterns follow the edge of the blade and usually turn back toward the tang at the point. In this instance, however, the turn-back *(kaeri)* is lacking.
   5) Wavy *(midare-komi)*. This type has a wavy tempered line on the point.
   6) Flame *(kaen)*.
   7) Solid temper *(ichi-mai)*. The point area is tempered thoroughly.
   8) Straight turn-back *(kaeri-tsuyoshi)*.
   9) Long turn-back *(kaeri-fukashi)*.
   10) Short turn-back *(kaeri-asashi)*.

2. DIVIDING LINE OF SURFACE AND POINT (YOKOTE). (Fig. 9.)

3. RIDGE LINE (SHINOGI). This line will not be found on *hira-zukuri* blades. Ridge lines are of two types (Fig. 13):

   1) Raised ridge line (*shinogi-takashi*).
   2) Flat ridge line (*shinogi-hikushi*).

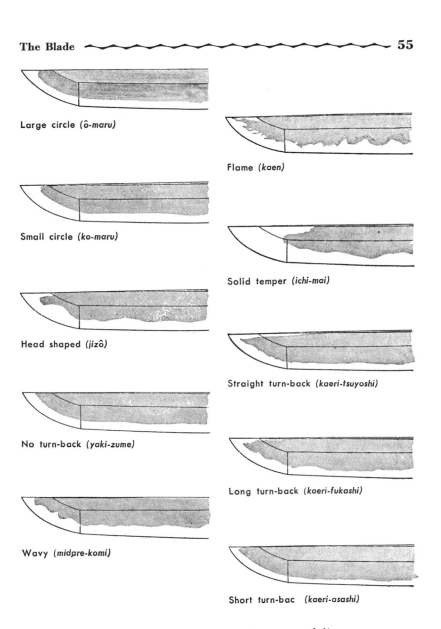

Large circle (ô-maru)

Flame (kaen)

Small circle (ko-maru)

Solid temper (ichi-mai)

Head shaped (jizô)

Straight turn-back (kaeri-tsuyoshi)

No turn-back (yaki-zume)

Long turn-back (kaeri-fukashi)

Wavy (midare-komi)

Short turn-bac (kaeri-asashi)

Fig. 12. *Points classified by tempered lines.*

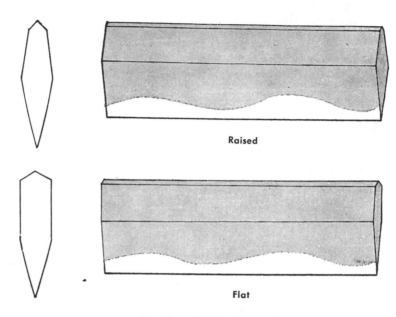

Raised

Flat

Fig. 13. *Ridge lines.*

4. UPPER SURFACE OR RIDGE AREA (SHINOGI-JI). Some smiths made swords with a wide upper surface; others, however, produced swords having the ridge line closer to the back (top) ridge (Fig. 14).

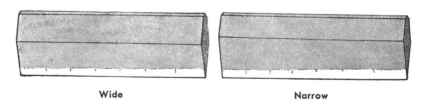

Wide　　　　　　　　Narrow

Fig. 14. *Upper surface or ridge area.*

5. SURFACE (JI) AND SURFACE DECORATION. Some blades have grooves *(hi)*, carvings *(horimono)*, and inscriptions *(bonji or kanji)* on the surface and upper surface *(shinogi-ji.)*

a. Grooves. Originally grooves were made to prevent the sword from bending and to lessen weight. However, grooves gradually came to be regarded as pure decoration. Grooves can be classified generally into eight shapes (Fig. 15), of which types (4) to (8) are commonly found on short swords:

1) Wide groove *(bo-hi)*.
2) Two narrow grooves *(futasuji-hi)*.
3) Wide and narrow grooves *(bo-hi ni tsure-hi)*.
4) Short groove *(koshi-hi)*.
5) Two short grooves *(gomabashi)*.
6) Joint-end twin grooves *(shobu-hi)*.
7) Joint-end irregular double grooves *(kuichigai-hi)*.
8) Halberd grooves *(naginata-hi)*.

Groove ends can be described in four ways (Fig. 16), of which types (1) and (2) are commonly found on blades made by smiths of the Old Sword period:

1) Chiselled through *(kaki-toshi)*.
2) Chiselled halfway *(kaki-nagashi)*.
3) Round end *(maru-dome)*.
4) Square end *(kaku-dome)*.

A groove tip extending past the *yokote* is called *hisaki-agari;* a groove tip stopping short of the *yokote* is called *hisaki-sagari*. The area in the upper surface not chiselled out is called *chiri*. A groove may have *chiri* on both sides *(ryo-chiri)* or only on one side *(kata-chiri)* (Fig. 17).

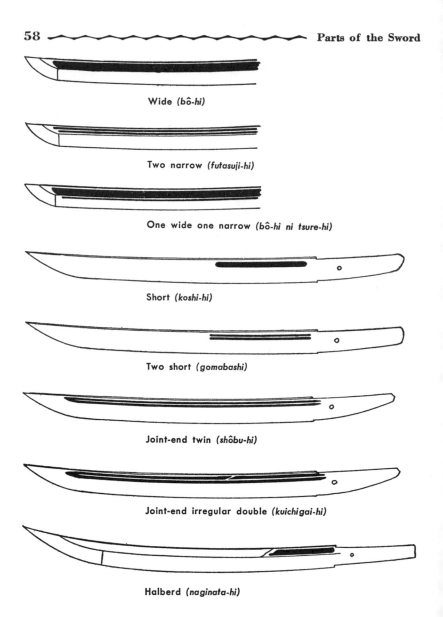

Wide (bô-hi)

Two narrow (futasuji-hi)

One wide one narrow (bô-hi ni tsure-hi)

Short (koshi-hi)

Two short (gomabashi)

Joint-end twin (shôbu-hi)

Joint-end irregular double (kuichigai-hi)

Halberd (naginata-hi)

Fig. 15. *Grooves.*

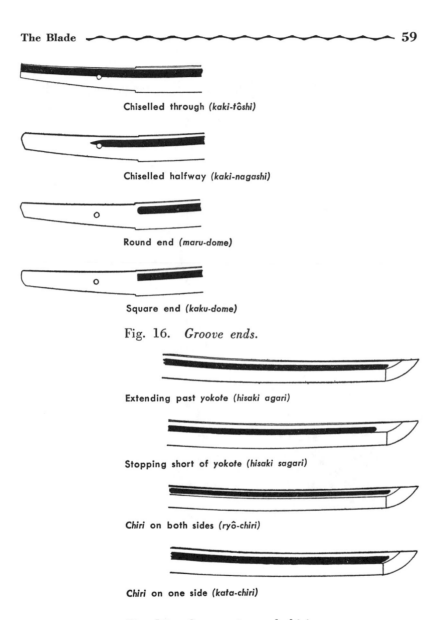

Chiselled through *(kaki-tôshi)*

Chiselled halfway *(kaki-nagashi)*

Round end *(maru-dome)*

Square end *(kaku-dome)*

Fig. 16. *Groove ends.*

Extending past *yokote (hisaki agari)*

Stopping short of *yokote (hisaki sagari)*

Chiri on both sides *(ryô-chiri)*

Chiri on one side *(kata-chiri)*

Fig. 17. *Groove tips and* chiri.

b. Carvings and inscriptions. These are also regarded as decorative refinements, although they were formerly thought to have religious significance. However, a sword is not necessarily a good sword merely because it has carvings or inscriptions on its surface or upper surface. As is often the case, many engravings are counterfeit, that is, they were added long after the sword was made, often to hide scars or defects of the blade.

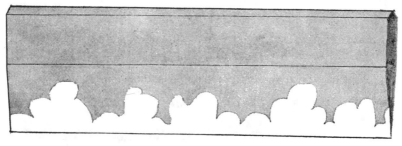

Nioi line

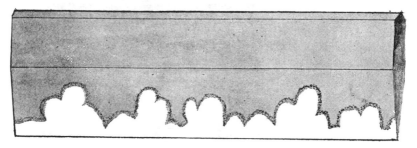

Nie line

Fig. 18. Nioi *and* nie.

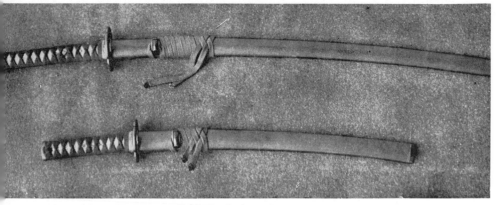

Plate 10. *A set of swords in* buke-zukuri *mount-ings. Top:* daito. *Bottom:* wakizashi. *Sometimes a* tanto *was used in place of a* wakizashi.

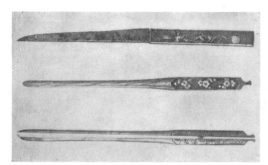

Plate 11. *Top:* kozuka (*utility knife*). *Middle:* kogai (*skewer*). *Bottom:* wari-bashi (*split chopsticks*).

Plate 12. Shira-saya (*plain wood scabbard*).

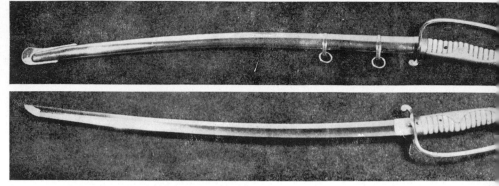

Plate 13. Kyu-gunto (*proto-army sword*). *A true samurai sword. Top: with the scabbard. Bottom: without the scabbard. Note the irregular tempered line on the blade.*

Plate 14. *Police or parade saber. Top: with scabbard. Bottom: detail of blade. Note the symmetrical wavy plated pattern.*

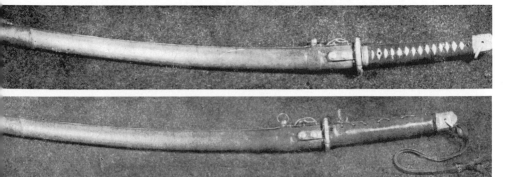

Plate 15. Shin-gunto (*neo-army swords*).
Top: Scabbard covered with leather. Hilt bound with cords. Bottom: Hilt and scabbard covered with leather.

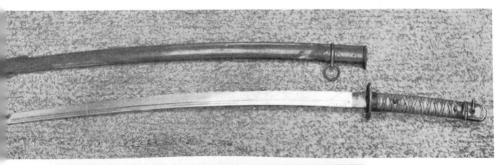

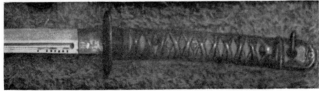

Plate 16. *A* shin-gunto (*neo-army sword*) *issued by the government. Detail shows the Arabic numerals on the ridge area.*

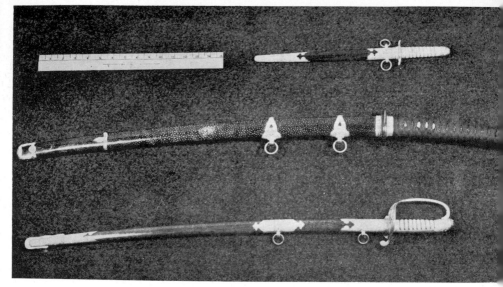

Plate 17. Kaigunto (*naval swords*). *Top: short sword. Middle: long sword.* Note the close resemblance to the jindachi-zukuri *and* shin-gunto *mountings.* The scabbard is dark blue. *Bottom: long sword.* Note resemblance to the police saber.

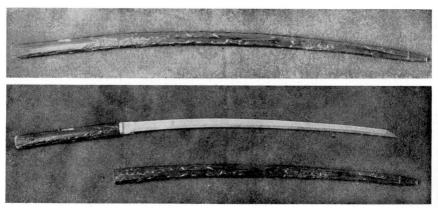

Plate 18. Shikomi-zue (*sword cane*).

6. TEMPERED LINE (YAKI-BA). The tempered line is a continuous straight or wavelike line running the length of the blade. As it is the hardest portion of the steel, it takes on a white color when skillfully polished. Such tempered lines represent the most beautiful feature of samurai swords and are the most important item in their appraisal.

a. Nioi and nie. The narrow misty-white line bordering the tempered edge of a blade between the tempered and untempered surface is caused by *nioi*. *Nioi* is a mixture of comparatively fine-grain martensite and troostite and is caused by slow quenching. *Nioi* always follows the true shape of the tempered-line pattern; however, due to polishing, it is difficult to discern. The best way to discern *nioi* is to hold a well-polished sword pointing toward a source of light at an angle of twenty to thirty degrees and look toward the light from a point about six inches above the blade. Some swords have a rather coarser-grain martensite on the tempered line. This is called *nie. Nie* also appears on the sword surface and is called by various other names depending on where and how it appears. *Nioi* and *nie* arc fundamentally the same thing; however, collectors divide tempered lines into *nioi* lines and *nie* lines (Fig. 18).

b. Types of tempered lines and their patterns. Tempered lines can be divided by their patterns into two general types: the straight line (patterns 1 to 8, below, and their combinations); and the wavy line (patterns 10 to 13 [*gunome*], 15 to 20 [*choji*], 9, 14, and 21 to 26 [miscellaneous], and their combinations). It is almost impossible to illustrate all the tempered-line patterns, especially of the *hitatsura* (full pattern), which assumes various shapes in various swords. The

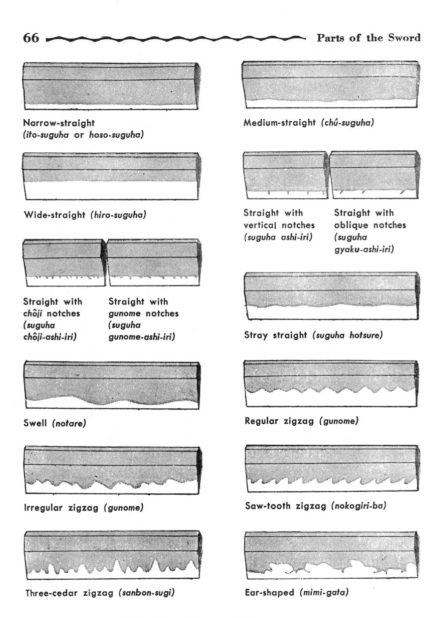

Narrow-straight
(ito-suguha or hoso-suguha)

Medium-straight (chû-suguha)

Wide-straight (hiro-suguha)

Straight with
vertical notches
(suguha ashi-iri)

Straight with
oblique notches
(suguha
gyaku-ashi-iri)

Straight with
chôji notches
(suguha
chôji-ashi-iri)

Straight with
gunome notches
(suguha
gunome-ashi-iri)

Stray straight (suguha hotsure)

Swell (notare)

Regular zigzag (gunome)

Irregular zigzag (gunome)

Saw-tooth zigzag (nokogiri-ba)

Three-cedar zigzag (sanbon-sugi)

Ear-shaped (mimi-gata)

Fig. 19.   Tempered-line patterns.

Clover-tree flower, mushroom-
shaped (chôji)

Double clover-tree flower
(jûka chôji)

Frog-shaped clover-tree flower
(kawazu chôji)

Oblique chôji (gyaku chôji)

Giant chôji (ô-chôji)

Small chôji (ko-chôji)

Dovetail (yahazu)

Box-shaped (hako-midare)

Billowing (dôran)

Bamboo-strip curtain (sudare-ba)

Chrysanthemum and river
(kiku-sui)

Full (hitatsura)

term *o-midare* (turbulent sea) is also used to describe the patterns of wavy lines. The following are some of the commoner tempered-line patterns (Fig. 19). Patterns marked with (*) are found only on swords of the New Sword period:

1) *Ito-suguha,* or *hoso-suguha* (narrow-straight)
2) *Chu-suguha* (medium-straight)
3) *Hiro-suguha** (wide-straight)
4) *Suguha ashi-iri* (straight with vertical notches)
5) *Suguha gyaku-ashi-iri* (straight with oblique notches)
6) *Suguha choji-ashi-iri* (straight with *choji* notches)
7) *Suguha gunome-ashi-iri* (straight with *gunome* notches)
8) *Suguha hotsure* (stray straight)
9) *Notare* (swell)
10) *Gunome* (regular zigzag)
11) *Gunome* (irregular zigzag)
12) *Nokogiri-ba* (saw-tooth zigzag)
13) *Sanbon-sugi* (three-cedar zigzag)
14) *Mimi-gata* (ear-shaped)
15) *Choji* (clover-tree flower, mushroom-shaped)
16) *Juka-choji* (double clover-tree flower)
17) *Kawazu choji* (frog-shaped clover-tree flower)
18) *Gyaku choji* (oblique *choji)*
19) *O-choji* (giant *choji)*
20) *Ko-choji* (small *choji)*
21) *Yahazu* (dovetail)
22) *Hako-midare* (box-shaped)
23) *Doran** (billowing)
24) *Sudare-ba** (bamboo-strip curtain)
25) *Kiku-sui** (chrysanthemum and river)
26) *Hitatsura* (full)

Smiths of various times and places used these tempered lines in many different kinds of combinations. But no one type of pattern was used exclusively by any given smith or school. This is especially true of the variety of patterns used by smiths of the Edo period. Chart I shows the general use of these patterns by smiths of various schools, locales, and periods.

7. BACK OR TOP RIDGE (MUNE). There are five types of back ridges (Fig. 20). Most common are (1) and (2), which are also referred to as *ihori-mune* or *gyo-no-mune*.

1) Low back *(mune-hikushi)*.
2) High back *(mune-takashi)*.
3) Double-ridge back *(mitsu-mune* or *shin-no-mune)*.
4) Round back *(maru-mune* or *so-no-mune)*.
5) Flat back *(hira-mune* or *kaku-mune)*.

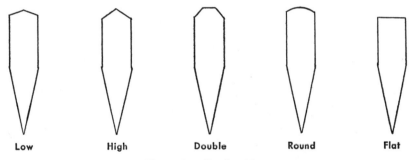

Low High Double Round Flat

Fig. 20. *Back ridges.*

8. CURVATURE (SORI). The curvature of a sword is measured at the top ridge. Generally speaking, curvatures are classified as deep or shallow. In most swords the point of deepest curvature appears at the center of the blade. This type is known as *torii* (Fig. 21). However, the Old Bizen School specialized in blades

Chart I

Use of tempered-line patterns in certain schools and areas by periods. Numbers in column one refer to pattern numbers as given in text.

PAT-TERN	NIE NIOI	PERIODS WITH CORRESPONDING SCHOOLS AND LOCALES					
		KAMAKURA & BEFORE	YOSHINO PERIOD	MUROMACHI PERIOD	MOMOYAMA PERIOD	EARLY EDO PERIOD	LATE EDO PERIOD
1-5, 8	Nie	Yamashiro Bizen Bitchû — Hôki	Yamato Hizen	Yamashiro Yamato Mino	Saga Yamato Mino	Osaka	Various
	Nioi	Bitchû Bizen	Bitchû Bingo	Mino Bingo	None		Various
6, 15-20	Nie	Yamashiro	Tajima	None	Saga	Saga	Various
	Nioi	Bitchû Bizen	Bitchû	None		Sekido Osaka	Various
7, 10-13	Nie	Etchû Mino & Others		Various			
	Nioi	Bizen		Mino Bizen	Mino & Others	Mino Bungo & Others	Various
9	Nie	None	Yama-shiro Sagami	Mino Ise	Kyoto Edo Osaka Fukui Saga Mino		Various
	Nioi	None	Bizen	Bizen Mino Ise	Mino	None	
O-MI-DARE	Nie	None	Etchû Sagami Chikuzen Yamashi-ro	Sagami	Kyoto Edo	Satsuma	Satsuma & Others
	Nioi	None		Sagami	None		
26	Nie	Yamashiro Sagami Etchû		Sagami	None		Various
	Nioi	None		Sagami Mino	Kyoto Fukui	None	
22-25	Nie	None			Kyoto	Osaka	Edo
	Nioi	None				Osaka	None

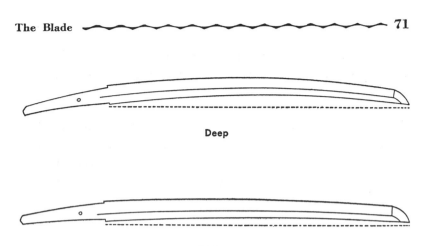

Deep

Shallow

Fig. 21. *Curvature,* torii *variety.*

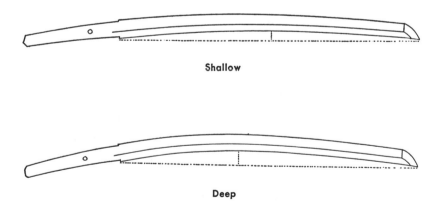

Shallow

Deep

Fig. 22. *Curvature,* koshi-zori *or* Bizen-zori.

whose greatest curvature was located much nearer the hilt (Fig. 22). This type of curvature was formally known as *koshi-zori* or *Bizen-zori*.

9. TANG (NAKAGO). The tang is the part of the blade which fits in the handle or hilt. Tangs are important in appraising samurai swords, particularly because they often reveal the date of a sword's construction and the identity of its maker. The tangs of swords made by any one school were usually similar.

a. Shapes of tangs (Fig. 23):
1) Pheasant thigh *(kiji-momo).* Tangs of this shape are found only among swords made during the Heian and Kamakura periods (794 to 1335).
2) Kimono sleeve *(furi-sode).* Swords, especially shorter blades, made during the Kamakura and Yoshino periods (1192 to 1383) often had tangs of this type.
3) Ship bottom *(funa-gata).* Tangs of this shape are often found among swords of the Soshu School.
4) Fish belly *(tanago-bara).* Tangs of this shape are found chiefly among swords of the Old Sword period (900 to 1530). The following often made blades with tangs of this shape: many smiths of Sagami Province (Soshu); smiths of the Heian-jo Branch of Yamashiro Province; Muramasa and others of Ise Province; Chika-shige (Shimobara) in Musashi Province.

b. Shape of tips of tangs (Fig. 24):
1) Double-beveled tip *(kuri-jiri* or *hira-yamagata).* This tip has a shape similar to that of a chestnut *(kuri)* and is the most commonly found tip in all periods.

Plate 19. *A tang with four rivet holes.*

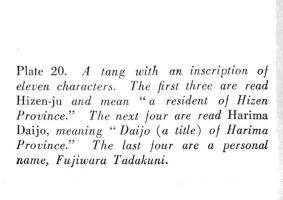

Plate 20. *A tang with an inscription of eleven characters. The first three are read* Hizen-ju *and mean "a resident of Hizen Province." The next four are read* Harima Daijo, *meaning "Daijo (a title) of Harima Province." The last four are a personal name,* Fujiwara Tadakuni.

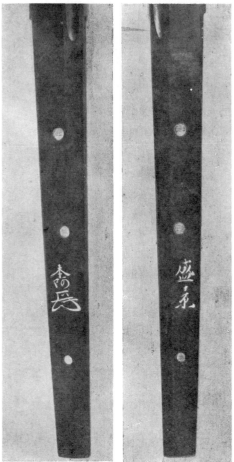

Plate 21. *A blade which has lost its original tang due to shortening and has been identified by the Honnamis, a famous family of sword appraisers. The illustration on the left shows their official signature, in gold inlay. The inscription on the reverse side of the same blade (right) gives the name of Morikage, a smith of Bizen Province, as the maker of the blade.*

Plate 22. *The result of a cutting test inscribed in gold inlay on a tang. Upper right:* Kanbun yo-nen go-gatsu saku-jitsu *(fourth year of Kanbun, fifth month, first day, or May 1, 1664). Middle:* Yamano Kauemon *(surname and middle name),* roku-ju-shichi sai *(age sixty-seven),* Nagahisa *(name of the tester). The bottommost character is the tester's sign. Upper left:* mitsu-do setsudan *(three bodies with one stroke).*

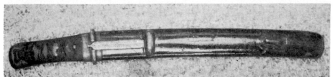

Plate 23. Tanto *illustrating scabbard pockets. The upper sword has a* kozuka *in its pocket. The bottom sword has a set of* wari-bashi.

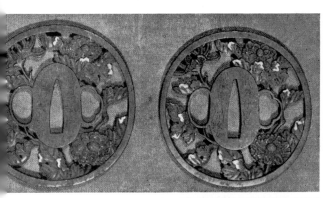

Plate 24. *A set of perfectly paired* tsuba *for a* daito *and a* wakizashi *by Ito Masakata, of Musashi Province, c. 1750. Openwork design in iron.*

Plate 25. Tsuba *with inlaid design of dragon. Note the signature of the maker between the main hole and the hole on the right.*

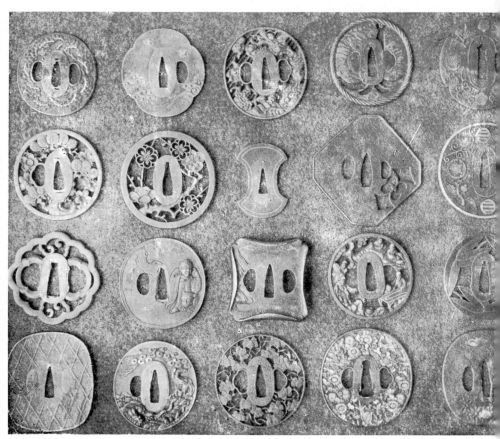

Plate 26. *A collection of* tsuba.

More sharply curved U-shaped tips are known as *taka-yamagata* or *fuka-kuri-jiri*.

2) Uneven U-shaped tip *(ha-agari kuri-jiri)*. The point of deepest curvature appears closer to the back edge of the tang.

3) Single-bevelled tip *(kata-yamagata)*. This tip is also known as *iri-yamagata*.

4) V-shaped tip *(kengyo)*. This tip was very common in the New Sword period (1531 to 1865). However, Masamune and Sadamune, of Sagami Province, Moritaka, of Chikuzen Province, and some smiths of Yamashiro and Kaga provinces used this tip in the Old Sword *(Koto)* period.

5) Square tip *(kiri or kaku-ichi-monji)*. Tangs with this tip are very common among the blades made by smiths of the Hosho Branch of Yamato Province in the Kamakura period (1192 to 1335). Also, they are common on blades which have been shortened.

c. File marks on tangs (yasuri-me). The file marks on swords of the Old Sword period are not clear, because of their great age. In other swords, however, file marks can be clearly recognized. File marks can be classified as follows (Fig 25), of which (1) to (3) were common on swords of all times, while (6) to (9) were used only on *shinogi-zukuri* (ridge line) swords:

1) Horizontal *(kiri, yoko, or ichi-monji)*.

2) Slightly slanting to the left *(kosuji-chigai or katte-sagari)*.

3) Slanting left *(suji-chigai)*.

4) Greatly slanting left *(o-suji-chigai)*. This file mark was

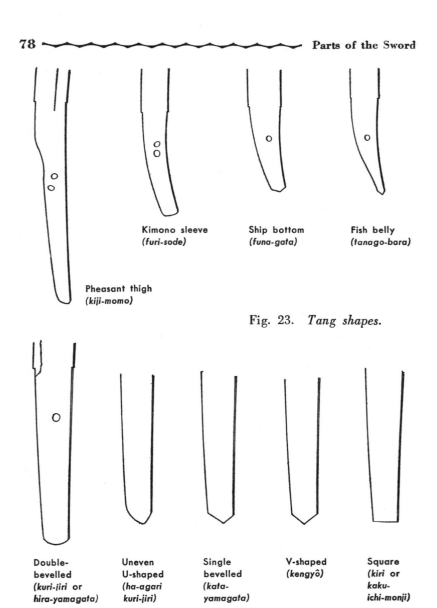

Kimono sleeve
(furi-sode)

Ship bottom
(funa-gata)

Fish belly
(tanago-bara)

Pheasant thigh
(kiji-momo)

Fig. 23. Tang shapes.

Double-
bevelled
(kuri-jiri or
hira-yamagata)

Uneven
U-shaped
(ha-agari
kuri-jiri)

Single
bevelled
(kata-
yamagata)

V-shaped
(kengyô)

Square
(kiri or
kaku-
ichi-monji)

Fig. 24. Shapes of tang tips.

chiefly used by the smiths of the Aoe Branch of Bitchu Province and the Sa Branch of Chikuzen Province.

5) Slanting right *(katte-agari)*.
6) Horizontal with leftward-slanting ridge area *(kiri-suji-chigai* or *shinogi-suji-chigai)*.
7) Slanting left with horizontal ridge area *(shinogi-kiri-suji-chigai)*.
8) V-shaped *(taka-no-ha)*. This mark was commonly used by smiths of Yamato and Mino provinces in the Old Sword period (900 to 1530). The smiths of Mino used it even in the New Sword period (1551 to 1865).
9) Inverted V *(gyaku-taka-no-ha)*.
10) Checked *(higaki)*. Smiths of Yamato and Mino provinces and the Naminohira Branch of Satsuma Province used these marks extensively in the Old Sword period (900 to 1530).
11) Full dress *(kesho-yasuri)*. These marks were used only by the smiths of the Edo period (1605 to 1668) and after.
12) Shaved *(sensuki)*. Some of the tangs of swords made before the twelfth century were shaved rather than filed.

d. Rivet hole in the tang (mekugi-ana). Many swords have more than one rivet hole, this being necessary in order to fit the tang into the mounting or to shorten the over-all length of the sword (Plate 19). From this it may generally be assumed that swords with two or more rivet holes are old. Bamboo rivets (pegs) are ordinarily used.

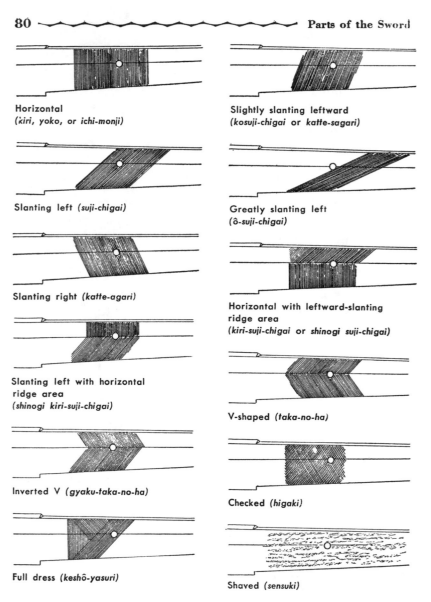

Horizontal
(kiri, yoko, or ichi-monji)

Slightly slanting leftward
(kosuji-chigai or katte-sagari)

Slanting left (suji-chigai)

Greatly slanting left
(ô-suji-chigai)

Slanting right (katte-agari)

Horizontal with leftward-slanting
ridge area
(kiri-suji-chigai or shinogi suji-chigai)

Slanting left with horizontal
ridge area
(shinogi kiri-suji-chigai)

V-shaped (taka-no-ha)

Inverted V (gyaku-taka-no-ha)

Checked (higaki)

Full dress (keshô-yasuri)

Shaved (sensuki)

Fig. 25.　File marks on tangs.

e. Inscriptions on tangs. Tangs may contain one or more of the following inscriptions (Plate 20):

1) First name of the smith.
2) Full name of the smith with or without his title.
3) Place.
4) Date.
5) Name of person ordering the sword.
6) Name of owner.
7) Name of co-worker.
8) Crest.
9) Good-luck saying or verse.
10) Age of the smith.
11) Name of steel used. Swordsmith Yasutsugu (c. 1700), of Echizen Province, stated that he made his swords with imported steel, chiefly wootz steel from India.
12) Name of the shrine or temple to which the sword was dedicated.
13) Data concerning the sword's shortening, such as date, name of original maker, smith who shortened it, place, etc.
14) Signature of the appraiser and name of assumed maker in gold or silver inlay or written in gold dust or in lacquer (Plate 21).
15) Result of cutting test. These cutting tests were unique, both in the way they were conducted and in the objects cut in the tests. There was a group of professionals who tested the sharpness of swords by cutting helmets, copper plate, oak poles, sheaves of straw with bamboo centers, and even, in the Edo period, condemned criminals and corpses. The testers kept close records of each test.

The record included such data as the name of the tester,
name of the witness, the date, and how many corpses
were cut with one stroke (Plate 22).

However, all tangs do not give this information. Some give
names, but they have been falsified. At present, the majority
of swords with the famous Masamune inscription are regarded
as imitations. Then too, since there were as many as thirteen
thousand swordsmiths in the course of Japanese swordmaking
history, it frequently happened that there were duplications in
names, particularly where the craft was handed down from
generation to generation in one family or from master to pupil.
For example, in Bizen there were seventy smiths of varying
skills who had the name of Sukesada (祐定).

The village of Osafune, in Bizen Province, was known for
its swordsmiths. One day Kanemitsu, one of the town's leading
smiths, was enjoying a moment of rest in his shop. He suddenly
found himself listening intently to the sound of the chisel of
his neighbor in the shop next door.

Angrily he arose, dashed next door, and seized the sword
on which the other smith had been chiseling a name.

"You were putting my name on that sword," said Kanemitsu.

The other smith admitted that he had been doing so and
apologized. "How did you know?" the guilty one asked. "Were
you watching?"

"No," answered Kanemitsu, "but I was listening. You used
a greater number of strokes than was necessary if you had been
writing your own name."

(This legend comes from the smiths of Bizen Province.)

It is obvious that counterfeiting was not always done long

after a sword was made. Smiths often used friends' names; apprentices used masters' names; and sons often used their fathers' names.

MOUNTINGS

Mountings include all the fittings and furniture of the sword exclusive of the blade (Figs. 26 and 27). Mountings are classified as follows:

Scabbard   Guard   Hilt

Fig. 26.   *Mountings.*

1. SCABBARD (SAYA). The scabbard is made of wood. Its primary purpose is to protect the blade. Usually it is lacquered or inlaid. Some scabbards have pockets (Plate 23) for a *kozuka* (utility knife), a *kogai* (skewer), or *wari-bashi* (split chopsticks) between the *tsuba* (guard) and the *kurigata* (cord knob).

2. GUARD (TSUBA). The guard protects the palm of the hand when holding the sword. It is made of steel, copper, silver, or some other metal. There are many people who collect *tsuba* because of the beautiful craftsmanship displayed in their construction (Plates 24, 25, 26). Also, there are some books whose sole purpose is to describe and comment about *tsuba*. *Tsuba*

usually have patterns or designs on both sides. The front side has a more decorative design and sometimes contains the maker's signature. The back side is usually less decorative. When mountings are assembled, the *tsuba* should be placed so that the front side faces toward the hilt. In addition to a wedge-shaped hole for the insertion of the tang, there are sometimes one or two extra holes to permit the insertion of a *kozuka*,

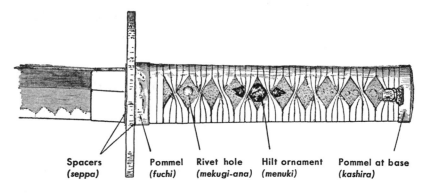

Spacers	Pommel	Rivet hole	Hilt ornament	Pommel at base
(seppa)	(fuchi)	(mekugi-ana)	(menuki)	(kashira)

Fig. 27.   *Hilt and portion of blade.*

kogai, or *wari-bashi*. A hole for a *kozuka* is always located on the left side of the main hole, when looking at the *tsuba* from the front with the pointed end of the main hole upwards. Extra holes are sometimes filled up with metal after the *tsuba* has been manufactured (Plate 27).

3. HILT OR HANDLE (TSUKA).   The tang of the blade is fitted in the hilt. The hilt is made of wood, has pommels on both ends, and is wrapped in ray skin and taped (Plate 28 and Fig. 27). There are several types of tapes used for binding the hilt. Some are made of silk, leather, or cotton and may

Plate **27**. Tsuba *showing an extra hole filled with gold. Sometimes, as in this case, a portion of the main hole is also filled with metal. This is done in order to fit the* tsuba *to a particular tang.*

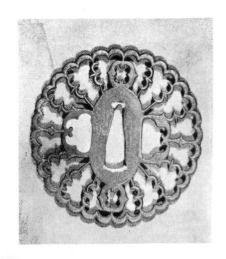

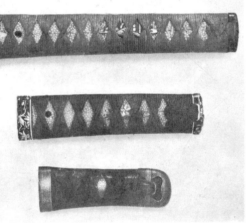

Plate 28. *Hilts for* buke-zukuri *mountings. Top: for a* daito. *Middle: for a* wakizashi. *Bottom: for a* tanto.

Plate 29. Habaki (*collar*).

Plate 30. Seppa (*spacer*).

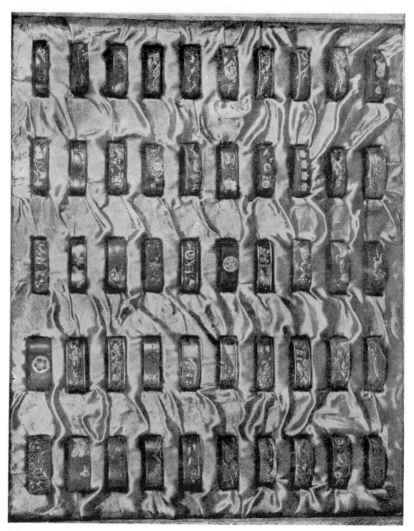

Plate 31. *A collection of* fuchi *and* kashira (*pommels*).

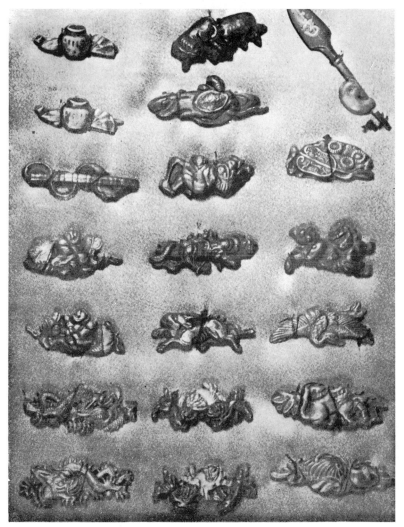

Plate 32. *A collection of* menuki (*hilt ornaments*).

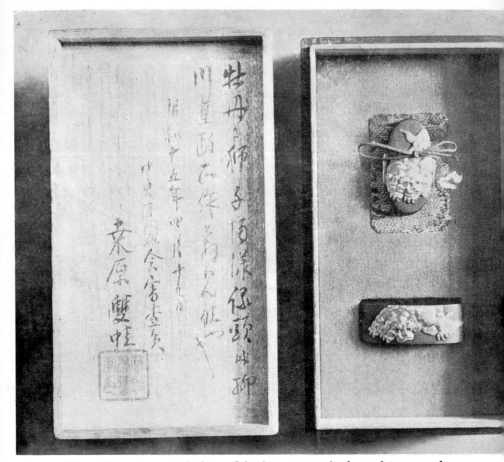

Plate 33. *A set of* fuchi *and* kashira, *properly housed in a wooden box. The inscription on the inside of the cover is an affidavit by Yojiro Kuwahara stating that this set is the authentic work of Master Naomasa Yanagawa.*

be either broad flat tape or cords wound in sets. Also, there are various ways of binding the tape. Some of the *jindachizukuri* mountings or the short sword *(tanto)* have hilts without binding called *hari-menuki* or *uki-menuki* (plugged-in hilt ornaments).

4. COLLAR (HABAKI). In order to prevent the blade from rattling in the scabbard, it is inserted in a wedge-shaped collar. A properly made collar wedges firmly inside the mouth of the scabbard to prevent the blade from rattling and from slipping accidentally out of the scabbard (Plate 29).

5. SPACERS OR WASHERS (SEPPA). (Plate 30 and Fig. 27).

6. POMMEL OR METAL SLEEVE (FUCHI). (Plate 31 and Fig. 27).

7. RIVET HOLE OF THE HILT (MEKUGI-ANA). (Fig. 27).

8. HILT ORNAMENTS (MENUKI). A hilt has a pair of *menuki*. Some of the pairs have identical designs, but some consist of companion or counterpart designs (Plate 32).

9. POMMEL AT BASE (KASHIRA). There are many people who collect pommels *(kashira* and *fuchi)* and hilt ornaments *(menuki)* because of their fanciful designs, just as there are many who collect guards *(tsuba)* (Plate 33).

4

Blade Shape, Construction, and Grain

BLADE SHAPE

THE SHAPES of the common samurai-sword blades are of the following types (Fig. 28), of which (1) to (7) have ridge lines, while (8) is without ridge line.

1) *Shinogi-zukuri.* This, the most common type, is found in the majority of long swords *(daito)*.
2) *Kanmuri-otoshi.*
3) *Unokubi-zukuri.* This and the preceding type are found in short swords *(tanto)*, chiefly among those made by smiths of the Yamato and allied schools after the late Kamakura period.
4) *Shobu-zukuri.* Blades of this type are generally short. They were popular in the Muromachi period.
5) *Moro-ha.* This type is found in the *tanto* and dates from the mid-Muromachi period. Straight blades of this

type with two cutting edges, known as *ken,* are very
scarce. Most *tanto* blades of the *ken* type were converted
from blades of spears *(yari).*

6) *Kata-kiri-ba.* Blades of this type are generally short.
They were popular in the late Kamakura and the Momo-
yama period.

7) *Kata-shinogi.* Blades of this type are generally short.
Excellent *kata-shinogi* blades are very rare.

8) *Hira-zukuri.* This is the most common type for short
blades.

Samurai-sword blades are commonly divided into the *hira-
zukuri* type (without ridge line) and the *shinogi-zukuri* type
(with ridge line). Chart II lists existing blades of this type,
according to their length and periods.

CHART II

EXISTING HIRA-ZUKURI AND SHINOGI-ZUKURI BLADES

PERIOD WHEN MADE	OVER 2 SHAKU		1 TO 2 SHAKU		UNDER 1 SHAKU	
	HIRA-ZUKURI	SHINOGI-ZUKURI	HIRA-ZUKURI	SHINOGI-ZUKURI	HIRA-ZUKURI	SHINOGI-ZUKURI
HEIAN (794 TO 1191)	None	Some	None	None	None	None
KAMAKURA (1192 TO 1335)	None	Many	Very Few	Very Few	Many	Some
YOSHINO (1336 TO 1383)	Very Few	Many	Some	Some	Many	Some
MUROMACHI (1384 TO 1574)	Very Few	Many	Some	Many	Many	Some
AZUCHI-MOMOYAMA (1575 TO 1605)	Very Few	Many	Some	Many	Some	Some
EDO (1606 TO 1868)	Very Few	Many	Some	Many	Some	Some

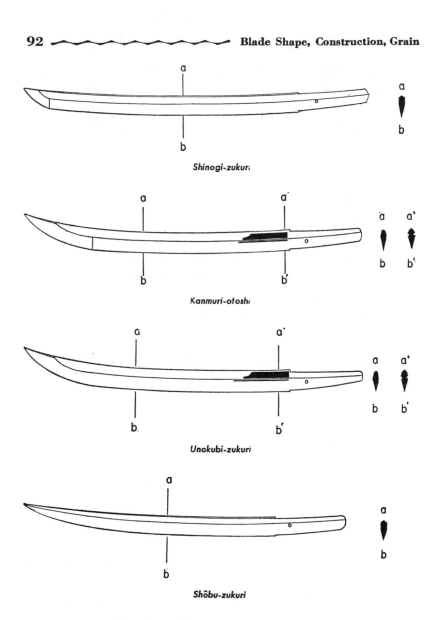

Fig. 28. *Shapes of common blades.*

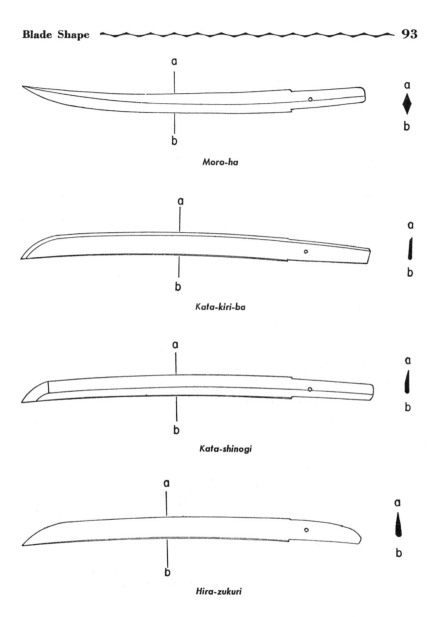

Moro-ha

Kata-kiri-ba

Kata-shinogi

Hira-zukuri

BLADE CONSTRUCTION

Cross sections of blades (Fig. 29) reveal the following types of construction *(kitae)*:

1) *Maru-gitae.* This type of construction, with one grade of steel. was used for mass production. Smiths of the New Sword period and those who used imported steel often employed this construction. Swords of this type usually reveal a smooth, grainless appearance on their surfaces.

2) *Wariba-gitae.* Harder blade-steel is applied to the blade, giving a better construction than (1).

3) *Makuri-gitae.* In this type the relatively soft core is surrounded by hard steel.

4) *Hon-sanmai-awase-gitae.* The soft core portion and the harder blade steel are covered by skin steel.

5) *Shiho-zume-gitae.* This type is the same as (4), except for the addition of back steel.

There are other types of cross sections, but discussion of them

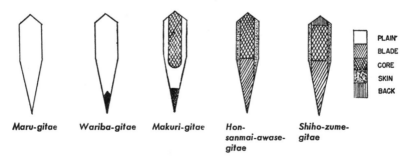

Maru-gitae Wariba-gitae Makuri-gitae Hon-sanmai-awase-gitae Shiho-zume-gitae

PLAIN
BLADE
CORE
SKIN
BACK

Fig. 29. *Cross sections showing blade construction.*

is outside the scope of a handbook. Although it is not easily evident from external appearance, the better the sword, the more complicated is its construction.

GRAIN

Before the sword assumes its final form, the metal is heated, stretched, and folded as many as twenty times. Thus, at its completion, fine layers appear on its ridge area and surface. The pattern these layers asume is called the grain *(hada)*. By the time the steel has been folded fifteen times, there will be 32,768 layers of steel. These layers form beautiful patterns visible only when the sword is skillfully polished. Some swords may not show a clear-cut single pattern but a mixture of two or more patterns. Also, some smiths used artificial methods to produce beautiful patterns or grains without folding the steel many times. In general, these patterns or grains are of the following types (Fig. 30):

1) Plain or no grain *(muji)*. These are commonly seen in *maru-gitae* swords of the New Sword period (1530 to 1868) and in swords of the Modern Sword period (since 1868).
2) Straight grain *(masame-hada)*.
3) Wood or wood-vein grain *(itame-hada)*.
4) Burl grain *(mokume-hada)*.
5) Curved grain *(ayasugi-hada)*.

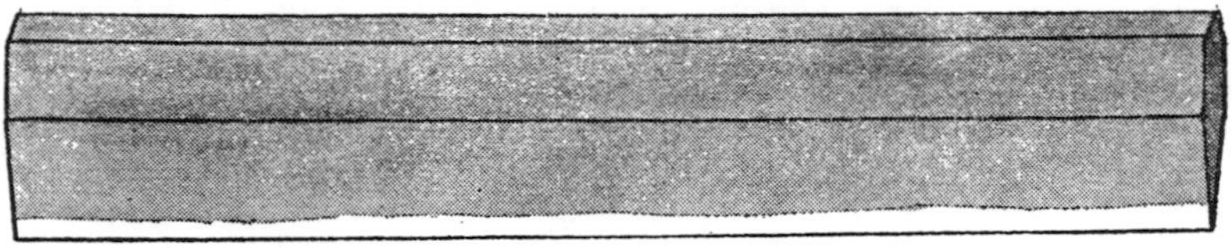

Plain or no grain (*muji*)

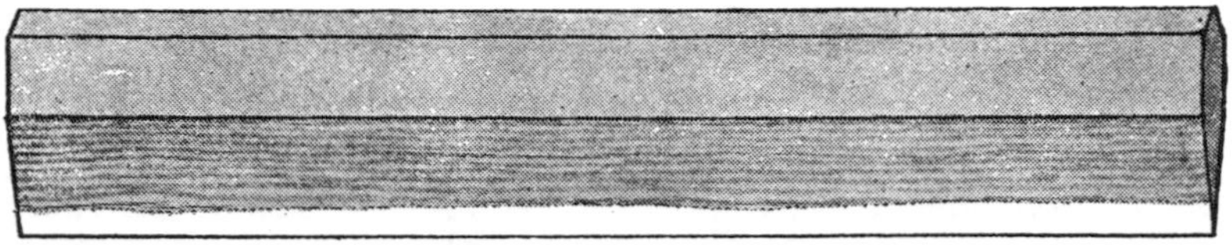

Straight (*masame-hada*)

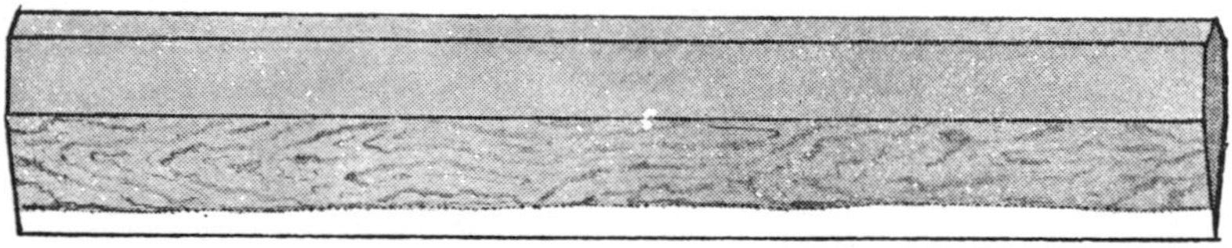

Wood (*itame-hada*)

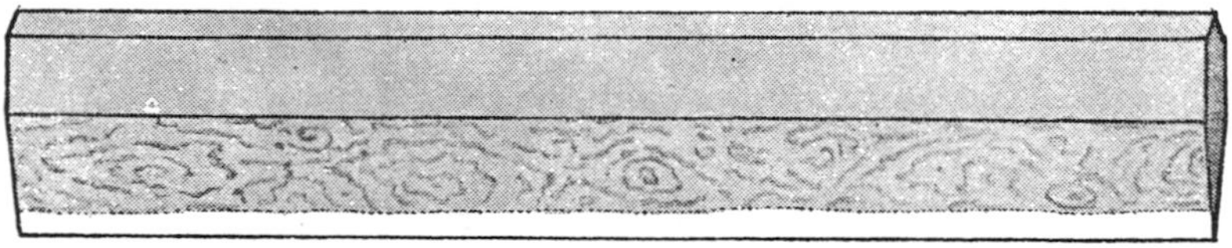

Burl (*mokume-hada*)

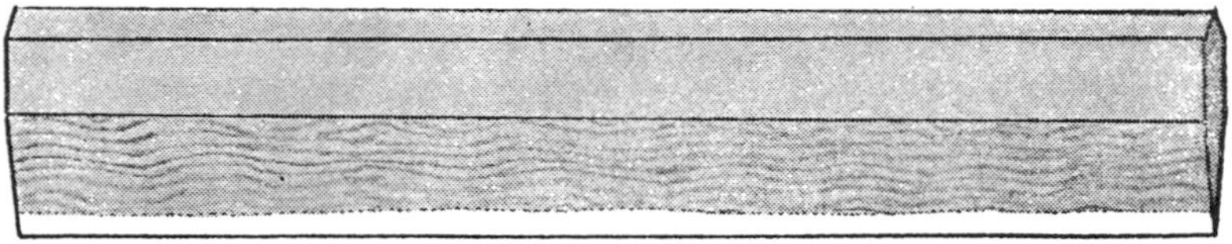

Curved (*ayasugi-hada*)

Fig. 30. *Blade grains.*

5

The Making of the Sword

WHEN THE THRUSTING action of the sword was replaced by
the cutting action, the swordsmiths endeavored to construct
swords whose blades would have uniform cutting efficiency
throughout their length. They discovered, through trial and
error, that a sword with a razor-sharp blade very often broke
off when used against armor. On the other hand, an unbreaka-
ble blade made of soft steel would bend. Another problem
was to make the sword sufficiently light for use in combat.
A weight of two or three pounds was found to be the most
satisfactory.

Since the earliest days of the Old Sword period, each school
of swordsmiths kept its own peculiar techniques of manufacture in the strictest confidence possible. These secrets were
handed down from master to apprentice or from father to son
by oral methods coupled with actual demonstrations. This desire
to guard secrets prevented rapid progress in the art.

The early swordsmiths left no written records of their find-
ings or their methods; and since no modern instruments were
available to measure either the hardness or the temperature
of steel, such factors were described by references to natural
phenomena. For example, "Heat the steel at final forging until

it turns to the color of the moon about to set out on its journey across the heavens on a June or July evening" (old calendar); or, "After the final forging, place the sword in water which has a temperature of water in February or August" (old calendar). They believed that water temperature in February and August was the same. Thus, when a swordsmith inscribed the month of manufacture on the sword, he generally used either February or August, regardless of the time of year the sword was actually made.

The great master of the New Sword period Suishinshi Masahide (1750 to 1825) made an intensive study of the old masters, and it is largely through his efforts that we are able to learn something of the ancient methods.

At first the swordsmith himself refined the steel from sand ores. However, beginning about 1450, the steel mills took over the job of refining and smeltering, and the quality of swords generally declined. After 1600 imported steel was used extensively by several smiths.

There are many methods of making swords. For the sake of brevity, only the principal steps are outlined here. This will give the reader a general idea of how swords are made. (See Plates 34 to 48 for a pictorial account of the making of the sword.)

Several pieces of metal are heated, stretched, and folded lengthwise. This heating and folding lengthwise is repeated many times. When the metal is malleable, it is pounded and beat upon until it is sufficiently tempered. The pieces of metal are gradually fashioned into a blade, but not until the entire process has been repeated from six to fifteen times. The smith quite often will put the steel through this cycle as many as thirty times.

Another and more complicated method is as follows. The pieces of steel are heated, pounded lengthwise, then folded lengthwise. The smith then pounds the steel out into a wide piece, folds this wide piece in half, pounds it into a long piece once more, and repeats the whole process.

Each time a piece is folded, the smith must exercise great care to see that all air and dirt are excluded. If he fails to do so, the sword will break in combat. Also, an extraordinary amount of skill is required to produce the proper degree of hardness. As described under Blade Construction, different grades of steel of varying hardnesses obtained through the above method are used.

A paste is made of clay, powdered grinding stone, charcoal, and other elements. This paste is spread over the sword blade, which is baked for its final tempering. After it attains a proper temperature, it is quenched in water of suitable temperature.

It is fitting to say a few words here about the attitude taken by the swordsmith toward his work and the atmosphere in which he worked. Men of every occupation in Japan had their own particular patron deity to which they looked for help and guidance. The swordsmith was no exception. In each forge there was a deity shelf, before which prayers were offered prior to starting and during work on each sword. The swordsmith was sincere in his work, for he believed that he had spiritual assistance.

After the smith engraved his signature, the blade was transferred to the hands of the polisher. The polisher, using several grades of stones, polished the sword over a period of time, usually one to two weeks.

Meanwhile, separate artists, working on different parts of the swords, were busy at their assigned task (Fig. 31). The hilt ornaments, handle bindings, guards, and the sheaths were all made by individual craftsmen. Finally, with a great blending of the efforts of all concerned, the sword was ready for its wielder. Since World War II, specialization of this type is rapidly disappearing.

Fig. 31. *Polisher, scabbard-maker, and lacquerer: eighteenth century.*

Plate 34. *The master performs a symbolic act of purification by pouring cold water over his body.* (*This and the following fourteen plates, showing the making of a sword, are used through the courtesy of Master Tsunetoshi Miyaguchi and the Society for the Preservation of the Japanese Sword, National Museum, Tokyo.*)

Plate 35. *He offers a fervent prayer before the deity shelf of his forge.*

Plate 36. *Iron of suitable quality is heated and flattened. Then it is quenched and broken into pieces of approximately equal size.*

Plate 37. *These pieces are piled upon a spatula made of iron of the same quality.*

Plate 38. *The spatula and iron pieces are heated in the fire.*

Plate 39. *The iron is repeatedly heated and pounded until it becomes a solid piece.*

Plate 40. *The sakite (aids) help the master pound and fold the metal, repeatedly heating it, until its texture is even throughout and the degree of steel desired is obtained.*

Plate 41. *Two pieces of steel which have been processed separately are fitted together with borox to form core- and skin-steel. This process results in a* kobuse *type of construction.*

Plate 42. *Repeated pounding gradually results in a stick-shaped piece of metal.*

Plate 43. *The master shapes the metal into a rough blade with a special shaver (sen) and files.*

Plate 44. *A coating of clay has been applied and allowed to dry Here it is being partly scraped off in a prescribed manner to obtain the desired tempered pattern.*

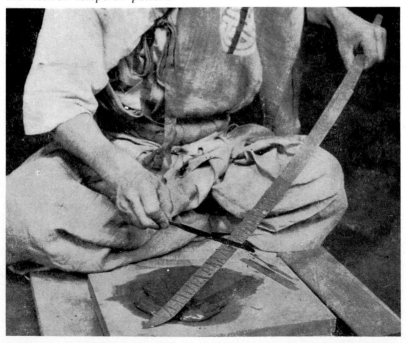

Plate 45. *The entire blade has been heated to a certain degree.*
Here it is about to be plunged into a tank of lukewarm water.

Plate 46. *Using*
a heated, grooved
block of copper,
the master corrects
the curvature of the
blade.

Plate 47. *A coarse stone is used to grind the blade into its final shape. Later it will be given to a specialist for polishing.*

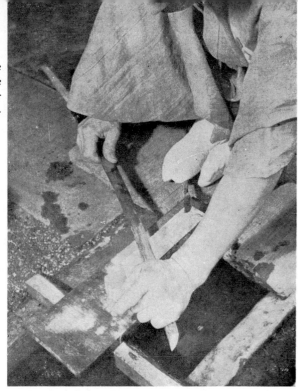

Plate 48. *The tang is finished last. Here the master inscribes his signature.*

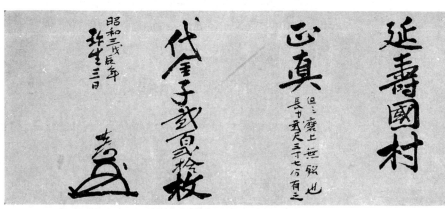

Plate 49. *A standard certificate issued by the Honnami family. Read from top to bottom and left to right. First line: Enju Kunimura (name of the smith); second line:* shoshin *("authentic," followed by a description of the blade in fine writing, stating that the blade had been shortened and had no inscription, its length being two* shaku *three* sun *seven* bu, or 2.35578 feet*). Third line:* daikin-su nihyaku-niju-mai *("price, 220 gold pieces"). The date, March 3, third year of Showa (1928), is written at the top of the fourth line, with the appraiser's signature at the bottom. The appraiser's seal is affixed exactly behind his signature on the reverse of the certificate.*

6

Inscriptions and Their Readings

ACCORDING TO THE JAPANESE manner of writing, characters appear one below the other. This must be kept in mind when referring to the following lists, because characters printed here vertically will appear horizontally in sword inscriptions. Another thing to remember is that the printed characters below may assume what appear to be quite different forms in actual inscriptions. This can be accounted for by deterioration caused by aging and by the highly individualistic manner of writing employed by many smiths.

PRONUNCIATION OF JAPANESE

Japanese is best spoken with no accent at all and in a near monotone. Vowels are always pronounced separately, even if two or more appear together. For example, *aoi* is pronounced ah-oh-ee; Osafune: oh-sah-foo-neh; Masamune: mah-sah-moo-neh; Etchū: et-choo. Long vowels should be carefully given their full value. For example, Ómi: oh-oh-me. There are five vowels in the Japanese language, pronounced as follows:

a	as in	father
i		unique
u		rude (but without rounding the lips)
e		met, bed
o		note

There are nineteen consonants in the Japanese language:

k, s, sh, t, ch, ts, n, h, f, m, y, r, w, d, b, p, g (like ng in sing), z (like ds in loads), j (like dg in judge)

Commonly Used Characters

One of the biggest problems for the Caucasian student of the sword is the recognition of the thousands of different characters which are commonly used in inscriptions. Even a well-educated Japanese may have difficulty reading such inscriptions and may occasionally misread them. For example, Kanemitsu (盍光 c. 1346) is known among Japanese as Ó-Ganemitsu (Great Kanemitsu). However, in this case the prefix ô does not mean "great" but was derived from the word uo, which means "fish." This misnomer arose because Kanemitsu's way of writing kane (盍) was similar to the character for fish (魚).

The following are some of the most common characters as they appear in one or more ways of writing. The Romanized readings given are those used by the smiths:

一 一 元 元   ICHI   one
first (year)
January

二 二 貳 弍   NI   **two**
second (year)
February

三 三 参   SAN   three
third (year)
March

四 四 二   SHI   four
fourth (year)
April

五 圡   GO   five
fifth (year)
May

六 仝   ROKU   six
sixth (year)
June

七 七   SHICHI   seven
seventh (year)
July

八 八   HACHI   eight
eighth (year)
August

九 九   KU   nine
ninth (year)
September

十 十 拾 拾	JYÛ	ten tenth (year) October
二 月 日	NI-GATSU-HI	one day in February
二 月 吉 日	NI-GATSU KITSU-JITSU	one lucky day in February
八 月 日	HACHI-GATSU HI	one day in August
八 月 吉 日	HACHI-GATSU KITSU-JITSU	one lucky day in August
秋 秋 秌	AKI	autumn
有 有 冇	ARI	presence
在	ARI	existence
俻 別	BISHÛ	Bi Provinces; Bizen, Bitchû, Bingo

偷 州	**BISHÛ** (*continued*)
近 近 迩 近	**CHIKA** near
親 觀 覩	**CHIKA** intimate
藤 原	**FUJI-WARA** a surname
籘 原	
房 房 房 房	**FUSA** tassel
春 春	**HARU** spring
治 沼	**HARU** govern
繁 繁	**HAN, SHIGE** prosperous

平 平 平 平	HEI TAIRA	flat a surname
廣 廣 廣	HIRO	broad
弘 弘 弘	HIRO	propagate
弘 弘		
久 久 久	HISA	lasting
寶	HÔ	treasure
雕	HORI	carve
歐 同 作	HORI-DÔSAKU	engravings by the same person
彫 物	HORI-MONO	engraving

刻 物			KIRI-MONO	engravings
切 物				
住 住 住			JÛ	resident of
搽 搽 拷 搽			JÔ	a title
景 景 景 景			KAGE	shadow
金 金			KIN, KANE	gold, money, metal
兼 兼 兼 兼			KANE	combine
魚 魚 魚 魚				
魚 魚 魚 魚				

包 包 包
巳 包 包　　　　KANE　　　wrap

勝 勝 勝
勝 猪　　　　KATSU　　　victory

帠 彪 彪 虖　　　KO, TORA　　tiger

是 是　　　　KORE　　　this

國 國 國 國
國 國 國 国
朋 図 図 国　　　KUNI　　　country, province

国 囯

KUNI
(*continued*)

正 正 正 正

MASA   right

正 正 正

政 政 政

MASA   government

政 政

昌 昌 昌

MASA   clear

道 道 逍

MICHI, DÔ   road

路 路

MICHI   road

源 源 源

MINAMOTO   a surname

源 源	MINAMOTO (*continued*)	
光 光 光 光 光	MITSU	light
明 明	MEI, MYÔ	bright
咸 咸 咸 咸 咸	MORI	full measure
守 守 守 守 守 守	MORI KAMI	defend a title
元 元 元	MOTO, GAN	first

元 元 | MOTO, GAN
(*continued*)

以メ ・ソ 以 | MOTTE | with

扗 村 | MURA | village

宗 宗 宗
宗 宗 | MUNE | reverent

旨 旨 | MUNE | sentiment

長 長 長
長 長 | NAGA, CHÓ | long

永 永 永 | NAGA, EI | lasting

仐	永			**NAGA** *(continued)*	
真	真	真		**NAO, SANE**	straight
直	直				
年	牟	年		**NEN**	year
秊	秂				
信	信	信	信	**NOBU**	trust
則	則	則		**NORI**	rule
則	則	昮			
法	法	法		**NORI**	law

於 於 於			OITE	at
扲 扲 扲				
長 舩			OSA-FUNE	Osafune Village
長 舩				
長 舩				
長 舩				
来			RAI	come
了 了 了			RYÔ	complete
負 負 負 欠			SADA	upright

先 先 先	SAKI	tip
左 左 左	SA	left
實	SANE	real
千 千 千	SEN	thousand
重 重 重 重	SHIGE	heavy
取 持	SHOJI	possession of
取 抱		
州 列 州 州	SHÛ	a province
列 凡 凡		

介 介   SUKE   a title

助 胁 助   SUKE   aid

� 助

祐 祐   SUKE   aid

橘 橘 擒 橘   TACHIBANA   a surname

忠 忠 忠   TADA, CHÛ   loyalty

忠 忠

隆   TAKA   prosperous

高 高   TAKA   high

武 武				TAKE	fierce
爲 烏 為 為				TAME	for the sake of
照 照 照 照				TERU	shine
輝 輝				TERU	shine
友 友 友				TOMO	friend
友 友					
倫 倫 倫				TOMO, RIN	code
俀 俀 俊				TOSHI	clever
次 次 次				TSUGU, JI	following

沼 吹	TSUGU (*continued*)	
継 継 継	TSUGU	continue
後 従		
作 作 作	TSUKURU	make
作 作		
造 造 造	TSUKURU	make
造 造 造		
製	TSUKURU, SEI	make
之 之 之	KORE	this

之 之 之   KORE
    (*continued*)

繩 繩 綱 繩   TSUNA   rope

恒 恒   TSUNE   constant

常 常   TSUNE   constant

氏 氏   UJI, SHI   a family, a suffix
                                       to a surname

寫 寫   UTSUSU   copy

若 若 若   WAKA   young

安 安 安 安   YASU, AN   peaceful

安 安 安

康 康	YASU	peaceful
義 義 義 義 義 義	YOSHI, GI	duty
吉 吉 吉 吉 吉	YOSHI	good luck
行 行 行 行 行 行	YUKI	go
幸 幸 幸	YUKI, YOSHI	happiness

Japanese Eras

The era during which a sword was made is often inscribed on the tang. Listed below in chronological order are the Japanese eras from 1053 to the present day. The number after the era name shows its duration in years, but one unit does not necessarily indicate a full calendar year. For example, because the last year of the Taisho era ended in mid-December, the next era (Showa) had only a few days in its first year, according to the Christian calendar. The year given merely indicates the year in which the era began.

Era names were often changed by the ruling emperor to commemorate an important event or to try to dispel bad luck. During a sixty-year period beginning in 1332, there were two imperial courts, the northern and the southern. Eras marked with (*) were designated by the northern court.

天 喜	Tenki	5	1053	康 和	Kôwa	5	1099
康 平	Kôhei	7	1058	長 治	Chôji	2	1104
治 暦	Jiryaku	4	1065	嘉 承	Kashô	2	1106
延 久	Enkyû	5	1069	天 仁	Tennin	2	1108
承 保	Shôho	3	1074	天 永	Ten-ei	3	1110
承 暦	Shôryaku	4	1077	永 久	Eikyū	5	1113
永 保	Eiho	3	1081	元 永	Gen-ei	2	1118
應 德	Ôtoku	3	1084	保 安	Hoan	4	1120
寛 治	Kanji	7	1087	天 治	Tenji	2	1124
嘉 保	Kaho	2	1094	大 治	Daiji	5	1126
永 長	Eichô	1	1096	天 承	Tenshô	1	1131
承 德	Shôtoku	2	1097	長 承	Chôshô	3	1132

保	延	Hoen	6	1135	嘉	祿	Karoku	2	1225
永	治	Eiji	1	1141	安	貞	Antei	2	1227
康	治	Kôji	2	1142	寬	喜	Kanki	3	1229
天	養	Tenyô	1	1144	貞	永	Jôei	1	1232
久	安	Kyûan	6	1145	天	福	Tempuku	1	1233
仁	平	Ninpei	3	1151	文	曆	Bunryaku	1	1234
久	壽	Kyûju	2	1154	嘉	禎	Katei	3	1235
保	元	Hogen	3	1156	曆	仁	Ryakunin	1	1238
平	治	Heiji	1	1159	延	應	En-ô	1	1239
永	曆	Eiryaku	1	1160	仁	治	Ninji	3	1240
應	保	Ôho	2	1161	寬	元	Kangen	4	1243
長	寬	Chôkan	2	1163	寶	治	Hôji	2	1247
永	萬	Eiman	1	1165	建	長	Kenchô	7	1249
仁	安	Nin-an	3	1166	康	元	Kôgen	1	1256
嘉	應	Kaô	2	1169	正	嘉	Shôka	2	1257
承	安	Shôan	4	1171	正	元	Shôgen	1	1259
安	元	Angen	2	1175	文	應	Bun-ô	1	1260
治	承	Jishô	4	1177	弘	長	Kôchô	3	1261
養	和	Yôwa	1	1181	文	永	Bun-ei	11	1264
壽	永	Juei	2	1182	建	治	Kenji	3	1275
元	曆	Genryaku	1	1184	弘	安	Kôan	10	1278
文	治	Bunji	5	1185	正	應	Shôô	5	1288
建	久	Kenkyû	9	1190	永	仁	Einin	6	1293
正	治	Shôji	2	1199	正	安	Shôan	3	1299
建	仁	Kennin	3	1201	乾	元	Kengen	1	1302
元	久	Genkyû	2	1204	嘉	元	Kagen	3	1303
建	永	Ken-ei	1	1206	德	治	Tokuji	2	1306
承	元	Shôgen	4	1207	延	慶	Enkei	3	1308
建	曆	Kenryaku	2	1211	應	長	Ôchô	1	1311
建	保	Kenpô	6	1213	正	和	Shôwa	5	1312
承	久	Shôkyû	3	1219	文	保	Bunpô	2	1317
貞	應	Jôô	2	1222	元	應	Genô	2	1319
元	仁	Gennin	1	1224	元	享	Genkyô	3	1321

正	中	Shôchû	2	1324	嘉	吉	Kakitsu	3	1441
嘉	曆	Kareki	3	1326	文	安	Bun-an	5	1444
元	德	Gentoku	2	1329	寶	德	Hôtoku	3	1449
元	弘	Genkô	3	1331	享	德	Kyôtoku	3	1452
正	慶	*Shôkei	2	1332	康	正	Kôshô	2	1455
建	武	Kenmu	2	1334	長	祿	Chôroku	3	1457
延	元	Engen	4	1336	寬	正	Kanshô	6	1460
曆	應	*Ryakuô	4	1338	文	正	Bunshô	1	1466
興	國	Kôkoku	6	1340	應	仁	Ônin	2	1467
康	永	*Kôei	3	1342	文	明	Bunmei	18	1469
貞	和	*Jôwa	5	1345	長	享	Chôkyô	2	1487
正	平	Shôhei	24	1346	延	德	Entoku	3	1489
觀	應	*Kan-ô	2	1350	明	應	Meiô	9	1492
文	和	*Bunwa	4	1352	文	龜	Bunki	3	1501
延	文	*Enbun	5	1356	永	正	Eishô	17	1504
康	安	*Kôan	1	1361	大	永	Taiei	7	1521
貞	治	*Jôji	6	1362	享	祿	Kyôroku	4	1528
應	安	*Ôan	7	1368	天	文	Tenmon	23	1532
建	德	Kentoku	2	1370	弘	治	Kôji	3	1555
文	中	Bunchû	3	1372	永	祿	Eiroku	12	1558
永	和	*Eiwa	4	1375	元	龜	Genki	3	1570
天	授	Tenju	6	1375	天	正	Tenshô	19	1573
康	曆	*Kôryaku	2	1379	文	祿	Bunroku	4	1592
弘	和	Kôwa	3	1381	慶	長	Keichô	19	1596
永	德	*Eitoku	3	1381	元	和	Genwa	9	1615
至	德	*Shitoku	3	1384	寬	永	Kan-ei	20	1624
元	中	Genchû	9	1384	正	保	Shôho	4	1644
嘉	慶	*Kakei	2	1387	慶	安	Keian	4	1648
康	應	*Kôô	1	1389	承	應	Shôô	3	1652
明	德	*Meitoku	4	1390	明	曆	Meiryaku	3	1655
應	永	Ôei	34	1394	萬	治	Manji	3	1658
正	長	Shôchô	1	1428	寬	文	Kanbun	12	1661
永	享	Eikyô	12	1429	延	寶	Enpô	8	1673

天 和	Tenwa	3	1681	享 和	Kyôwa	3	1801
貞 享	Jôkyô	4	1684	文 化	Bunka	14	1804
元 祿	Genroku	16	1688	文 政	Bunsei	12	1818
寳 永	Hôei	7	1704	天 保	Tenpô	14	1830
正 德	Shôtoku	5	1711	弘 化	Kôka	4	1844
享 保	Kyôhô	20	1716	嘉 永	Kaei	6	1848
元 文	Genbun	5	1736	安 政	Ansei	6	1854
寬 保	Kanpô	3	1741	萬 延	Man-en	1	1860
延 享	Enkyô	4	1744	文 久	Bunkyû	3	1861
寬 延	Kan-en	3	1748	元 治	Genji	1	1864
寳 曆	Hôryaku	13	1751	慶 應	Keiô	3	1865
明 和	Meiwa	8	1764	明 治	Meiji	44	1868
安 永	An-ei	9	1772	大 正	Taishô	14	1912
天 明	Tenmei	8	1781	昭 和	Shôwa	—	1926
寬 政	Kansei	12	1789				

THE ZODIACAL CYCLE

In addition to counting time by years, the Japanese also use a system similar to the zodiac. The symbols of this system often appear in sword inscriptions and are helpful in dating and identifying swords. Two sets of characters appear in the zodiacal cycle. The first set consists of ten ordinal signs, similar to our A B C, when used for enumeration. They are called: *kinoe; kinoto; hinoe; hinoto; tsuchinoe; tsuchinoto; kanoe; kanoto; mizunoe;* and *mizunoto.* The second set consists of twelve zodiacal symbols, named as follows: *ne,* rat; *ushi,* ox; *tora,* tiger; *u,* hare; *tatsu,* dragon; *mi,* snake; *uma,* horse; *hitsuji,* sheep; *saru,* monkey; *tori,* chicken; *inu,* dog; and *i,* hog. Each successive year in the cycle is designated by two characters, one from each of the two lists, taking the characters from each list in their regular order. Since one list contains only ten characters and the other twelve, this combining of the two lists produces a total of sixty different combinations, at which point the cycle is completed and the counting starts over again in the same manner. For example, the first fourteen years of the cycle are named as follows:

1	kinoe-ne	8	kanoto-hitsuji
2	kinoto-ushi	9	mizunoe-saru
3	hinoe-tora	10	mizunoto-tori
4	hinoto-u	11	kinoe-inu
5	tsuchinoe-tatsu	12	kinoto-i
6	tsuchinoto-mi	13	hinoe-ne
7	kanoe-uma	14	hinoto-ushi

The following list of *kinoe-ne* years covers approximately the last thousand years:

964	1324	1684
1024	1384	1744
1084	1444	1804
1144	1504	1864
1204	1564	1924
1264	1624	

Chart III gives the ordinal and zodiacal signs with their Japanese and Chinese readings. When the ordinal signs are used for enumeration, exclusive of their function as year-enumerators, their Chinese readings are employed.

Chart III

Readings for Ordinal and Zodiacal Signs

ORDINAL SIGNS			ZODIACAL SIGNS		
	JAPANESE READING	CHINESE READING		JAPANESE READING	CHINESE READING
甲	Kinoe	Ko	子	Ne	Shi
乙	Kinoto	Otsu	丑	Ushi	Chu
丙	Hinoe	Hei	寅	Tora	In
丁	Hinoto	Tei	卯	U	Bo
戊	Tsuchinoe	Bo	辰	Tatsu	Shin
己	Tsuchinoto	Ki	巳	Mi	Shi
庚	Kanoe	Kô	午	Uma	Go
辛	Kanoto	Shin	未	Hitsuji	Bi
壬	Mizunoe	Jin	申	Saru	Shin
癸	Mizunoto	Ki	酉	Tori	Yu
			戌	Inu	Jutsu
			亥	I	Gai

7

Care and Maintenance

ALTHOUGH THE PRIMARY function of the sword is that of a cutting weapon, the swords under consideration here should never be used to cut hard objects. Such an action would serve only to ruin the blade. Care should be exercised so as not to damage the tape or leather binding on the handle or to mar the mounting in any way. In the United States it is almost impossible to find an artisan who is capable of rebuilding a handle.

The beauty and value of the samurai sword rests chiefly on the excellence of its flawless polish. Since painstaking and delicate care must be taken to maintain the polish of the steel, the blade should never be touched with the hand. Such contact is not only dangerous but will also lead to eventual rusting. The best way to prevent rust is to keep the sword lightly oiled. It is better to use light-weight oil, since heavy-weight oil will soil the interior of the scabbard by causing dust to collect. If the sword is kept in a salty atmosphere, apply oil once a month. In mountainous regions apply oil once every three months. Before re-oiling the blade, wipe old oil from it with a soft fabric, such as facial tissue. Then sprinkle special oil-removing powder *(uchi-ko)* or talcum powder on the blade surface. Remove the powder by wiping gently with a clean tissue, then oil the blade with light, fine oil.

The importance of oiling the blade at regular intervals cannot be overemphasized, for it is the best way to prevent corrosion. There is hardly anyone in the United States qualified to polish swords or to make repairs on mountings. Should an amateur attempt to polish a sword himself, the result might be the complete ruination of the blade.

It is advisable not to use metal polish on the blade or on the metal mountings, especially the guard *(tsuba)*. Because the tang contains vital information about the maker, it should *never* be polished.

8

Appraisal and Value

THE STUDY AND ART of appraising is as old as the history of swords. Its art and secrets were handed down from master to apprentice by word of mouth, but even though written notes were made by some appraisers, they were kept in secret and very few are available at the present time. The first such notes are dated as early as 1315.

In the thirteenth century, a need for good appraisers arose, and the Honnami family began to specialize in the art. For generations thereafter, the Honnamis were official appraisers for the Toyotomi and the Tokugawa shogunates and issued certificates regarding the authenticity and history of swords (Plate 49). Generally these certificates are quite reliable, but during the course of time certificates for some swords have become interchanged with those of others. One may also come across swords with forged certificates. Unfortunately, the majority of the secret records of this family were destroyed in the Great Earthquake of 1923, and very few of their records were ever published. After the Meiji era there were many other appraisers, in addition to the Honnami family, who issued certificates.

It is advisable for sword owners to obtain complete information about their swords from a reliable expert. This is best accomplished by having him examine the sword. However, if the tang has an inscription, the information can be obtained through the mail by sending a rubbing *(oshigata)* of the tang along with other descriptions to the expert. The rubbing can be made by placing a piece of onionskin paper over the tang and rubbing it with a soft lead pencil held slantwise (Fig. 8). If the inscription contains the name of the maker, an appraiser can establish the authenticity of the sword quite easily. But when such names are lacking, an exhaustive study must be made. An examination of the following items will usually reveal the identity of the maker: curvature; color and grain of steel; tempered line on surface; ridge area (upper surface); shape of point; tempered line in point; ridge line; back (top) ridge; shape of tang; file marks on tang; other factors. There are many copies of older swords done by later smiths, but an expert can detect these forgeries quite easily. The imitations done by a smith's colleagues or students in his own time, however, are difficult to distinguish from authentic works.

At present in the United States there are no more than two or three expert samurai-sword appraisers, and hardly anyone qualified to repair mountings or make plain wood scabbards *(shira-saya)*. As a result, many valuable and famous swords lie neglected in attics, barns, and second-hand shops.

Throughout the course of time the value of swords has been subject to much fluctuation. During World War II they were in great demand and commanded high prices. However, with the end of the war the demand has decreased considerably, except among a small but avid group of collectors.

The value placed on most blades is largely determined by the reputation of the maker; age has little effect on worth. For example, a blade made in 1661 by Kotetsu (Musashi Province) commands several times the price of one made in 1368 by Kunimune (Etchu Province). Even among the swords of any one smith, however, value varies considerably depending on length and workmanship. The value of a sword with excellent engravings or forged by two or more smiths or with historical significance is often doubled.

There are no standard prices at the present time, but prewar standards may be used as a reference. The maximum price ranged from 20,000 to 30,000 yen ($5,000 to $7,500) in 1932. Such swords were generally six hundred to one thousand years old, had significant historical value, and were regarded as being practically in the category of national treasures. On the other hand, Japanese officers could buy sound samurai swords forged 150 to 300 years ago for 150 to 300 yen ($40 to $75).

Mountings have a value independent of the blade. Many swords have *tsuba* and handle-pommel ornaments *(menuki)* of gold and silver, but the amount or precious metal used in such ornaments is comparatively small and of insignificant value. They are prized more for their workmanship and artistic design. Some of them are valued at hundreds of dollars for their artistic worth alone.

9

Relative Point Values

In a handbook it is impossible to list the names of all recognized smiths. In Japan many books have been published solely for this purpose. Here, however, the subject will be covered only to the extent of indicating comparative point values for the more important smiths. Variable factors make it unfeasible to attempt to assign absolute values to smiths and their works in terms of good, better, best, or monetary value. The following list makes no such attempt, but is merely designed to give a relative basis for evaluating individual swords. The point values given apply to blades over two *shaku* in length, with normal, not embellished, mountings (furniture) included, and in perfect condition, i.e., properly polished and without defects. Swords under two *shaku* but over one *shaku* in length should be evaluated on a basis of one half the listed value. Evaluation of swords less than one *shaku* should be based on one-third the listed value. Blades which have defects or rust or are without authentic inscriptions or proper mountings should be reduced in value accordingly. Conversely, extravagant mountings will add to the listed point value.

The points were computed by the author on the basis of the comparative reputations of the swordsmiths and by careful examination of market bulletins, catalogs, auction results, and the like. It must be kept in mind that the points are merely relative. For example, a perfect sword by Akihiro (value of 100) would be of one half the value of a perfect sword by Choen (value of 200), and so on for any smith listed. Mountings, such as *tsuba*, have a market value independent of the blade.

Arabic numerals after the names indicate the number of smiths with the same names who worked concurrently or at approximately the same time in the same province. For example, there were six smiths by the name of Kanenaga (兼長) in Mino Province, two in Hoki, two in Iwami, three in Bizen, one in Settsu, one in Tamba, one in Hizen, one in Satsuma, and so on, at different times and of varying skills.

If you know that your sword was made by a smith called Kanenaga without knowing the Chinese characters with which it is inscribed, it may have been made by one of seventeen Kanenagas (兼長), or six Kanenagas (包長), or one Kanenaga (金長), or about fourteen Kanenagas (兼永), or about seventeen Kanenagas (包永), or others, between the dates 1200 to 1850.

Certain names with two popular pronunciations are listed twice. The year refers to the smith's approximate period of greatest productivity.

Name of Smith				Province	Year	Value
Akihiro	秋	廣	2	Sagami	1299	100
Akikazu	誠	和		Bizen	Present	5
Akikuni	顯	國		Nagato	1362	100
Akiyoshi	顯	吉		Nagato	1384	35
Akizane	章	實		Bizen	1207	150
Akizane	明	眞		Yamashiro	1596	15
Amafuji	天	藤		Yamato	750?	500
Amakuni	天	國		Yamato	700?	600
Arikuni	有	國		Yamashiro	1028?	140
Arimasa	有	正		Mutsu	970?	170
Arimitsu	有	光		Bizen	1394	15
Arinari	有	成		Kôchi	1012?	190
Aritsune	有	常		Shinano	1356	25
Asasuke	朝	助		Bizen	1184	150
Asatada	朝	忠		Mimasaku	1184	150
Asataka	朝	尊		Yamashiro	1818	10
Bokuden	卜	傳		Hitachi	1624	10
Chikafusa	近	房		Bizen	1220	150
Chikakage	近	景		Bizen	1318	130
Chikakane	近	包		Bizen	1184	145
Chikamura	近	村		Bizen	1303	130
Chikatada	近	忠		Bizen	1212	145
Chikatsugu	親	次	2	Bitchû	1278	140
Chôen	長	圓		Bungo	1184	200
Chôkichi Nagayoshi	長	吉		Yamashiro	1334	75
Chôkô Nagayuki	長	幸		Settsu	1658	30
Enshin	圓	眞		Tokyo	1870	5
Enshin	圓	眞		Tokyo	Present	5
Fujiie	藤	戶		Yamato	800?	190
Fuyuhiro	冬	廣		Wakasa	1444	10

Name of Smith				Province	Year	Value
Fuyuhiro	冬	廣		Wakasa	1661	10
Gassan	月	山		Uzen	1190?	90
Gisuke	義	助		Suruga	1444	10
Hankei	繁	慶		Musashi	1673	40
Harukuni	治	國		Settsu	1688	10
Hidechika	秀	近		Bizen	1350	35
Hidekage	秀	景		Bizen	1356	50
Hidemitsu	秀	光		Bizen	1384	30
Hidemori	秀	守		Bizen	1361	30
Hidenaga	秀	長		Izu	1428	15
Hidenori	秀	則		Bizen	1394	10
Hidesane	秀	實		Bizen	1350	50
Hidesuke	秀	助		Bizen	1384	25
Hidetsugu	秀	次		Bizen	1335	60
Hideyo	秀	世		Musashi	1844	10
Hideyoshi	英	義		Musashi	1844	10
Hirokane	弘	包		Yamato	1661	5
Hirokuni	廣	國		Aki	1688	5
Hiromasa	廣	正		Sagami	1375	15
Hiromasa	廣	政		Settsu	1683	10
Hiromitsu	廣	光	4	Sagami	1350	95
Hiromura	弘	村		Higo	1288?	140
Hironobu	廣	宣		Mino	1661	5
Hironobu	廣	信		Yamashiro	1684	5
Hiroshige	廣	重		Musashi	1684	5
Hiroshige	廣	重		Tôtômi	1684	5
Hirotaka	汎	隆		Chikuzen	1658	10
Hirotaka	廣	隆		Aki	1661	5
Hirotaka	廣	高		Settsu	1673	5
Hirotaka	廣	隆		Settsu	1804	5
Hirotsugu	廣	次		Sagami	1368	15
Hirotsune	廣	恒		Bizen	1234?	125

NAME OF SMITH				PROVINCE	YEAR	VALUE
Hiroyasu	弘	安		Chikuzen	1336	60
Hiroyuki	弘	幸		Yamashiro	1624	15
Hisakuni	久	國		Yamashiro	1199	195
Hisakuni	久	國		Tosa	1624	10
Hisakatsu	久	勝		Suô	Present	5
Hisamichi	久	道		Yamashiro	1688	10
Hisamitsu	久	光		Bizen	1387	15
Hisanobu	久	信		Yamashiro	1384	25
Hisatsugu	久	次		Bizen	1384	15
Hisayuki	久	幸		Musashi	1818	10
Hôju	寶	壽	4	Mutsu	1326	130
Ichijô	一	乘		Bingo	1394	50
Iemune	家	宗		Sagami	1329	60
Ienaga	家	永		Chikuzen	1504	20
Iesada	家	貞		Bizen	1345	45
Iesuke	家	助		Bizen	1350	25
Iesuke	家	助		Bizen	1394	75
Iesuke	家	助		Bizen	1394	15
Ietada	家	忠		Kaga	1615	5
Ietsugu	家	次		Bitchû	1210?	110
Ietsugu	家	次		Nagato	1661	5
Ippô	一	峯		Musashi	1684	10
Jinsoku	神	息		Buzen	987?	500
Jôshû	定	秀		Bungo	1160?	205
Jukaku	壽	格		Imba	1818	10
Jumyô	壽	命		Mino	1243	35
Kaboku	加	卜		Musashi	1648	10
Kagehide	景	秀		Bizen	1256	140
Kagehira	景	平		Kaga	1661	5
Kagekuni	景	國		Yamashiro	1222	150
Kagemasa	景	政		Bizen	1329	70
Kagemitsu	景	光		Bizen	1321	140

Name of Smith			Province	Year	Value
Kagemitsu	景光		Kaga	1362	15
Kagenaga	景長	4	Inaba	1303	130
Kagenori	景則		Bizen	1280 ?	115
Kageyasu	景安		Bizen	1280	130
Kageyori	景依	2	Bizen	1280 ?	125
Kaneaki	兼明		Tôtômi	1394	10
Kaneaki	包明		Yamato	1688	5
Kanechika	包近		Bizen	1220	150
Kaneharu	兼春		Kaga	1661	5
Kanehira	包平		Bizen	1074	205
Kanehiro	兼廣		Hizen	1661	5
Kanehisa	兼久		Mino	1368	15
Kanekage	兼景		Mino	1345	15
Kanekage	兼景		Mino	1688	5
Kanekiyo	包清		Yamato	1362	30
Kanekuni	包國		Yamato	1319	40
Kanekuni	兼國		Yamato	1368	35
Kanekuni	包國		Yamato	1596	10
Kanekuni	包國		Harima	1688	5
Kanekuni	包國		Yamato	1774	5
Kanekura	金藏		Mino	1681	5
Kanemaki	兼巻		Kaga	1624	5
Kanemichi	包道		Bizen	1220	150
Kanemichi	金道	10	Yamashiro	1592	5
Kanemichi	兼道		Yamashiro	1661	5
Kanemitsu	兼光		Mino	1352	15
Kanemitsu	兼光	2	Bizen	1356	130
Kanemitsu	兼光		Mimasaku	1684	5
Kanemori	包保		Settsu	1600	10
Kanemori	包保		Settsu	1661	10
Kanemoto	兼基		Mino	1444	45
Kanemoto	兼元		Mino	1457	50

NAME OF SMITH				PROVINCE	YEAR	VALUE
Kanemoto	兼	元		Mino	1624	5
Kanemune	包	宗		Yamato	1661	5
Kanenaga	兼	永		Yamashiro	1087	145
Kanenaga	包	永	4	Yamato	1288	145
Kanenaga	兼	長		Bizen	1346	95
Kanenaga	兼	長		Mino	1362	15
Kanenaga	兼	永		Mino	Present	5
Kanenobu	兼	延		Mino	1317	30
Kanenobu	兼	信		Mino	1352	30
Kanenobu	兼	信		Mino	1652	5
Kanenori	包	則		Echigo	1661	5
Kanenori	包	則		Musashi	Present	5
Kaneô	金	王		Yamato	1189?	100
Kanesada	包	貞		Yamato	1345	50
Kanesada	兼	定		Mino	1467	50
Kanesada	兼	定		Iwashiro	1624	5
Kanesada	包	定		Yamato	1661	5
Kanesada	兼	定		Mino	1673	5
Kanesada	包	貞		Settsu	1673	10
Kanesada	兼	貞		Mino	1681	5
Kanesada	兼	定		Iwashiro	1865	5
Kanesaki	兼	先		Inaba	1596	5
Kanesane	包	眞		Yamato	1362	35
Kaneshige	金	重	2	Mino	1319	100
Kaneshige	兼	重		Bizen	1334	100
Kaneshige	包	重		Settsu	1661	10
Kaneshige	兼	重		Musashi	1661	10
Kaneshige	金	重		Yamato	1804	5
Kanesue	包	末		Bizen	1220	150
Kanesuke	包	助		Bizen	1220	150
Kanesuke	包	助		Yamato	1362	30
Kanetomo	兼	友		Mino	1336	50

Name of Smith				Province	Year	Value
Kanetora	兼	虎		Shinano	1865	5
Kanetoshi	包	利		Yamato	1365	95
Kanetoshi	兼	利		Mino	1375	15
Kanetsugu	包	次	3	Yamato	1317	90
Kanetsugu	兼	次		Mino	1368	15
Kanetsugu	兼	繼		Mino	1368	15
Kanetsuna	包	綱		Settsu	1624	5
Kanetsune	兼	常		Mino	1394	10
Kanetsune	兼	常		Musashi	1684	5
Kaneuji	兼	氏		Mino	1320	160
Kanewaka	兼	若		Kaga	1596	10
Kaneyasu	兼	安		Bingo	1356	25
Kaneyoshi	兼	吉		Mino	1400 ?	40
Kaneyoshi	包	吉		Rikuzen	1624	5
Katsuie	勝	家		Kaga	1624	5
Katsukuni	勝	國		Kaga	1596	10
Katsumitsu	勝	光		Bizen	1429	15
Katsuyoshi	勝	吉		Ise	1624	5
Kazuhide	一	秀		Uzen	1818	5
Kijû	紀	充		Yamato	1688	5
Kikusaku	菊	作		Yamashiro	1220	300
Kinjû Kaneshige	} 金	重		Mino	1319	100
Kiyofusa	清	房		Sanuki	1300	30
Kiyohide	清	秀		Chikuzen	1818	5
Kiyohira	清	平		Sagami	1658	10
Kiyohira	清	平		Nagato	1716	5
Kiyokata	清	方		Satsuma	1744	5
Kiyomitsu	清	光		Bizen	1504	15
Kiyomitsu	清	光		Kaga	1661	5
Kiyomaro	清	麿		Musashi	1830	35
Kiyondo	清	人		Musashi	1861	10

Name of Smith				Province	Year	Value
Kiyonobu	清	信		Settsu	1661	5
Kiyonori	清	則		Bizen	1394	15
Kiyosada	清	貞		Suô	1345	25
Kiyosuke	清	左		Satsuma	1488	10
Kiyotsuna	清	繩	3	Suô	1335	35
Kiyozane	清	眞		Nagato	1331	10
Korekazu	是	一		Musashi	1661	10
Korekazu	是	一		Musashi	1861	10
Koresuke	是	助		Bizen	1264	150
Koretoshi	是	俊		Uzen	1861	5
Kotetsu	虎	徹		Musashi	1661	70
Kunifusa	國	房		Etchû	1394	15
Kunifusa	國	房		Iyo	1624	5
Kunihide	國	秀		Musashi	1818	10
Kunihira	國	平		Settsu	1673	5
Kunihira	國	平		Kaga	1688	5
Kunihira	國	平		Satsuma	1711	10
Kunihiro	國	廣		Sagami	1329	115
Kunihiro	國	弘		Chikuzen	1358	100
Kunihiro	國	廣		Yamashiro	1596	100
Kunihiro	國	廣		Iyo	1624	5
Kunihisa	國	久		Yamashiro	1345	55
Kuniie	國	家		Yamashiro	1184	150
Kunikane	國	包		Bizen	1219	170
Kunikane	國	包		Rikuzen	1661	10
Kunikane	國	包		Rikuzen	1688	5
Kunikane	國	包		Rikuzen	1704	5
Kunikiyo	國	清		Yamashiro	1207	150
Kunikore	國	維		Iyo	1661	5
Kunimasa	國	富		Hyûga	1681	5
Kunimasa	國	正		Higo	1381	15
Kunimasa	國	改		Yamashiro	1624	10

Name of Smith				Province	Year	Value
Kunimasa	國	正		Musashi	1688	5
Kunimasa	國	方		Ôsumi	1716	5
Kunimichi	國	路		Yamashiro	1661	25
Kunimichi	國	路		Yamashiro	1688	10
Kunimitsu	國	光		Yamashiro	1249	120
Kunimitsu	國	光	3	Sagami	1278	145
Kunimitsu	國	光		Yamashiro	1328	145
Kunimitsu	國	光		Bitchû	1352	25
Kunimitsu	國	光	2	Tajima	1365	100
Kunimitsu	國	光		Musashi	1684	5
Kunimori	國	盛		Mikawa	1394	15
Kunimori	國	護		Musashi	Present	5
Kunimune	國	宗	2	Bizen	1230	130
Kunimune	國	宗		Etchû	1368	15
Kunimune	國	宗		Echizen	1624	5
Kunimura	國	村		Higo	1356	120
Kuninaga	國	永		Yamashiro	1328	145
Kuninaga	國	長	3	Settsu	1329	100
Kuninaga	國	長		Echizen	1334	25
Kuninaga	國	長		Yamashiro	1362	45
Kuninobu	國	信		Yamashiro	1352	100
Kuninobu	國	信		Higo	1329	70
Kunisada	國	貞		Iyo	1342	25
Kunisada	國	貞		Settsu	1624	15
Kunisada Shinkai	國	貞		Settsu	1673	45
Kunisada	國	貞		Settsu	1688	15
Kunishige	國	重	3	Yamashiro	1334	115
Kunishige	國	重		Kôzuke	1368	25
Kunishige	國	重		Bitchû	1661	15
Kunishige	國	重		Bitchû	1661	10
Kunishige	國	重		Settsu	1673	5

NAME OF SMITH				PROVINCE	YEAR	VALUE
Kunisue	國	末		Yamashiro	1293	125
Kunisuke	國	資	2	Higo	1380	95
Kunisuke	國	助		Settsu	1624	10
Kunisuke	國	助		Settsu	1661	10
Kunisuke	國	助		Settsu	1673	10
Kunisuke	國	助		Musashi	1688	5
Kunitada	國	忠		Izumi	Present	5
Kunitake	國	武		Yamashiro	1624	5
Kuniteru	國	輝		Iyo	1661	5
Kuniteru	國	輝		Settsu	1681	15
Kunitoki	國	時	2	Higo	1339	125
Kunitomo	國	儔		Yamashiro	1655	35
Kunitomo	國	友		Yamashiro	1199?	185
Kunitora	國	虎		Settsu	1688	5
Kunitoshi	國	俊	3	Yamashiro	1293	150
Kunitoshi	國	俊		Tamba	1469	95
Kunitoshi	國	俊		Settsu	1870	5
Kunitsugu	國	次		Yamashiro	1311	150
Kunitsugu	國	次		Kii	1384	25
Kunitsugu	國	次		Etchû	1394	10
Kunitsugu	國	次		Mino	1460	15
Kunitsugu	國	次		Echizen	1615	5
Kunitsugu	國	次		Musashi	1661	5
Kunitsugu	國	次		Yamashiro	1624	5
Kunitsugu	國	次		Musashi	1624	5
Kunitsuna	國	綱		Yamashiro	1213	170
Kunitsuna	國	綱	2	Higo	1357	70
Kunitsuna	國	綱		Bizen	1362	35
Kunitsuna	國	經		Higo	1368	35
Kunitsuna	國	綱		Settsu	1681	5
Kuniyasu	國	安		Yamashiro	1207	170
Kuniyasu	國	安		Yamashiro	1220	95

Name of Smith			Province	Year	Value
Kuniyasu	國	泰	2	Higo	1310	100
Kuniyasu	國	安		Echizen	1352	25
Kuniyasu	國	奏		Higo	1394	10
Kuniyasu	國	安		Echizen	1394	10
Kuniyasu	國	安		Iwashiro	1615	10
Kuniyasu	國	安		Yamashiro	1661	35
Kuniyasu	國	康		Settsu	1688	10
Kuniyasu	國	安		Tôtômi	1818	10
Kuniyoshi	國	吉		Yamashiro	1247	145
Kuniyoshi	國	吉		Higo	1329	115
Kuniyoshi	國	義		Settsu	1661	5
Kuniyoshi	國	吉		Musashi	1764	5
Kuniyuki	國	行	2	Yamato	1248?	130
Kuniyuki	國	行	4?	Yamashiro	1293	150
Kuniyuki	國	幸		Settsu	1624	5
Kunizane	國	實		Tamba	1303	30
Kunizane	國	眞		Yamashiro	1312	85
Masaaki	正	明		Musashi	1861	10
Masachika	正	近		Bingo	1375	15
Masafusa	正	房		Satsuma	1648	10
Masahide	正	秀		Musashi	1804	25
Masahiro	正	廣		Bingo	1332	40
Masahiro	正	廣		Sagami	1375	15
Masahiro	正	廣		Hizen	1624	10
Masahiro	正	弘		Musashi	1658	10
Masahiro	正	廣		Hizen	1661	5
Masahiro	正	弘		Yamashiro	1661	15
Masahiro	正	廣		Hôki	1688	5
Masahiro	政	弘		Tôtômi	Present	5
Masaie	正	家	5	Bingo	1324	115
Masaie	政	家		Bingo	1338	35
Masaie	正	家		Bingo	1394	35

NAME OF SMITH			PROVINCE	YEAR	VALUE
Masakane	正	包	Hidachi	Present	5
Masakatsu	正	勝	Musashi	1661	5
Masakatsu	正	勝	Mito	Present	5
Masakiyo	方	清	Nagato	1688	5
Masakiyo	正	清	Satsuma	1711	35
Masakuni	正	國	Tamba	1350 ?	160
Masakuni	正	國	Higo	1596	5
Masamitsu	正	光	Yamashiro	1381	35
Masamori	正	守	Shimozuke	1624	5
Masamune	正	宗	Sagami	1326	300
Masamune Daruma	正	宗	Yamashiro	1352	60
Masamune	正	宗	Bingo	1362	25
Masamune	政	宗	Bingo	1455	15
Masanaga	正	永	Echizen	1394	15
Masanaga	政	長	Iwashiro	1624	5
Masanaga	正	永	Hizen	1624	5
Masanari	正	成	Bizen	1624	5
Masanobu	正	信	Echigo	1356	50
Masanori	正	則	Echizen	1652	5
Masanori	正	則	Satsuma	1716	5
Masanori	將	應	Musashi	1789	5
Masao	正	雄	Musashi	1861	10
Masashige	正	重	Ise	1384	30
Masashige	正	繁	Harima	1716	10
Masashige	正	重	Ise	1661	5
Masashige	政	重	Hizen	Present	5
Masatomo	正	全	Owari	1661	5
Masatoshi	正	俊	Ise	1368	25
Masatoshi	正	俊	Yamashiro	1596	15
Masatoshi	正	俊	Yamashiro	1661	5
Masatsugu	正	次	Satsuma	1661	5

Name of Smith				Province	Year	Value
Masatsugu	正	次		Musashi	1844	10
Masatsugu	正	次		Musashi	Present	5
Masatsuna	正	綱		Settsu	1624	5
Masatsune	正	恒	2	Bizen	1100?	205
Masatsune	政	常		Owari	1615	10
Masatsune	政	常		Owari	1624	10
Masayoshi	正	義		Musashi	1861	15
Masayoshi	正	吉		Musashi	1870	5
Masayoshi	正	幸		Satsuma	1789	10
Masazane	正	眞		Ise	1368	15
Masazane	正	眞		Bingo	1394	10
Masazane	正	眞		Yamato	1596	5
Michinaga	道	長		Iwashiro	1661	5
Mitsuchika	光	近		Bizen	1368	35
Mitsuhira	光	平		Musashi	1648	10
Mitsuhiro	光	弘		Bizen	1368	25
Mitsukage	光	景		Bizen	1384	30
Mitsukane	光	包		Ômi	1308	115
Mitsumasa	光	昌		Chikuzen	1681	5
Mitsumasa	光	將		Owari	1716	5
Mitsushige	光	重		Yamashiro	1330	110
Mitsutada	光	忠		Bizen	1238	170
Mitsutoshi	光	俊		Tajima	1394	10
Mitsutsugu	光	次		Bitchû	1303?	80
Morihide	盛	秀		Nagato	1804	5
Morichika	盛	近		Bizen	1362	30
Morifusa	盛	房		Mikawa	1688	5
Morihisa	守	久		Bizen	1361	30
Moriie	守	家		Bizen	1232	145
Morikage	盛	景		Bizen	1356	70
Morikage	守	景		Bizen	1362	45
Morikuni	盛	國		Chikuzen	1288	35

Name of Smith				Province	Year	Value
Morikuni	盛	國		Musashi	1661	10
Morikuni	護	國		Aki	Present	5
Morimasa	守	正		Kai	1624	5
Morimichi	盛	道		Owari	1661	5
Morimichi	盛	道		Owari	1681	5
Morimitsu	守	光		Bizen	1394	15
Morimitsu	盛	光		Bizen	1394	60
Morinaga	盛	永		Musashi	1661	5
Morinori	盛	則		Bizen	1394	15
Morishige	盛	重		Bizen	1308	35
Morisuke	守	助		Bizen	1352	30
Morisuke	守	助		Ômi	1394	10
Moritaka	盛	高	3	Chikuzen	1293	70
Moritoshi	盛	俊		Aki	Present	5
Moritsugu	守	次		Bitchû	1151	140
Moritsuna	守	繩		Hôki	990 ?	150
Moritsuna	盛	綱		Chikuzen	1278	45
Moriyoshi	守	吉		Etchû	1361	45
Moriyuki	守	行		Bizen	1335	60
Moriyuki	盛	行		Hizen	1596	5
Morokage	師	景		Bizen	1394	25
Moromitsu	師	光		Bizen	1394	50
Morozane	師	實		Bizen	1220	150
Morozane	師	實		Bizen	1368	45
Motochika	基	近		Bizen	1278	115
Motohira	元	平		Satsuma	1789	25
Motohiro	元	寛		Satsuma	1818	5
Motomasa	基	政		Bizen	1356	50
Motomitsu	基	光		Bizen	1380 ?	100
Motomune	元	宗		Bizen	1356	45
Motooki	元	興		Iwashiro	1804	5
Motosada	元	貞		Satsuma	1684	5

NAME OF SMITH				PROVINCE	YEAR	VALUE
Motoshige	元	重		Bizen	1304	140
Mototake	元	武		Satsuma	1789	10
Mototsugu	基	次		Sagami	1375	35
Mototsuna	基	綱		Bizen	1352?	60
Motoyasu	元	安		Tôtômi	1394	15
Motoyasu	元	安		Satsuma	1789	5
Motoyuki	本	行		Hizen	1661	5
Motozane	元	眞		Chikugo	1074?	170
Munechika	宗	近		Yamashiro	987?	300
Munechika	宗	近		Iga	1334	70
Munehiro	宗	寛		Musashi	1865	10
Munemitsu	宗	光		Bizen	1324	45
Munemitsu	宗	光		Bizen	1469	15
Munenaga	宗	長		Bizen	1222	130
Munenaga	宗	長		Settsu	1375	25
Munenaga	宗	長		Hyûga	1596	5
Munenaga	宗	長		Hizen	1596	15
Munenaga	宗	長		Hyûga	1596	5
Munenori	宗	則		Bizen	1350?	35
Muneshige	宗	重		Settsu	1661	5
Muneshige	宗	重		Harima	1661	5
Munetada	宗	忠		Tango	1334?	170
Munetaka	宗	隆		Hôki	1207	150
Munetaka	宗	隆		Iga	1362	35
Munetô	宗	遠		Bitchû	1230?	145
Munetsugu	宗	次		Hizen	1615	5
Munetsugu	宗	次		Musashi	1830	15
Muneyasu	宗	安		Bizen	990?	170
Muneyoshi	宗	吉		Bizen	1220	170
Muneyoshi	宗	榮		Harima	1661	10
Muneyuki	統	行	2	Bungo	1596	5
Muramasa	村	正		Ise	1362	85

NAME OF SMITH				PROVINCE	YEAR	VALUE
Muramasa III	村	正		Ise	1429	15
Myôju	明	壽		Yamashiro	1596	70
Nagakuni	長	國		Iyo	1661	5
Nagamichi	長	道		Iwashiro	1661	10
Nagamitsu	長	光	4	Bizen	1270	150
Nagamitsu II	長	光		Bizen	1288	140
Nagamitsu III	長	光		Bizen	1334	25
Nagamitsu	長	光		Yamashiro	1360?	55
Nagamori	長	守		Bizen	1317	60
Nagamori	長	盛		Bungo	1441	15
Nagamune	長	旨		Musashi	1673	15
Nagamune	長	宗		Musashi	1673	10
Naganao	長	直		Bizen	1362	70
Naganobu	長	信		Musashi	1830	10
Naganori	長	則		Bizen	1300?	90
Naganori	長	則		Bizen	1317	55
Nagashige	長	重		Bizen	1334	85
Nagasuke	長	助		Bizen	1220	150
Nagatsuna	長	綱		Bizen	1335	70
Nagatsuna	長	綱		Settsu	1661	5
Nagayoshi	長	吉		Yamashiro	1334	75
Nagayoshi	長	義		Bizen	1352	140
Nagayoshi	長	吉		Echigo	1362	35
Nagayoshi	長	吉		Yamashiro	1661	5
Nagayuki	長	幸		Settsu	1658	30
Naohide	直	秀		Musashi	1868	5
Naokatsu	直	勝		Musashi	1830	15
Naokatsu	直	勝		Musashi	1861	10
Naomichi	直	道		Yamashiro	1661	5
Naomune	直	宗		Bizen	1190	140
Naotane	直	胤		Musashi	1818	15
Naotsuna	直	綱	4	Iwami	1334	100

Name of Smith				Province	Year	Value
Nariie	成	家		Bizen	1352	35
Narimune	成	宗		Bizen	1199	130
Nichijô	日	乘		Bizen	1384	15
Nobufusa	信	房		Bizen	1069	205
Nobufusa	延	房		Bizen	1207	180
Nobufusa	信	房		Bizen	1220 ?	170
Nobufusa	信	房		Tôtômi	1596	5
Nobufusa	延	房		Owari	1681	5
Nobuie	信	舍		Owari	1772	5
Nobuhide	信	秀		Musashi	1861	10
Nobuhide	信	秀		Settsu	Present	5
Nobuhisa	信	久		Yamashiro	1368	35
Nobukane	信	包		Bizen	1219	30
Nobukane	信	包		Yamashiro	1368	75
Nobukuni	信	國	5	Yamashiro	1334	85
Nobukuni	信	國		Yamashiro	1394	45
Nobumasa	信	正		Bizen	1219	150
Nobumitsu	信	光		Bizen	1292	115
Nobumitsu	信	光		Chikuzen	Present	5
Nobunaga	信	長		Kaga	1394	15
Nobushige	信	重		Echigo	1381	15
Nobushige	宜	繁		Hizen	Present	5
Nobutaka	信	高		Owari	1615	10
Nobuteru	信	照		Owari	1688	5
Nobuyoshi	延	吉		Yamato	1317	70
Nobuyoshi	延	吉		Yamashiro	1688	5
Norifusa	則	房		Mimasaku	1334	140
Norifusa	則	房		Etchû	1624	5
Norihiro	則	弘		Yamato	1249	115
Norihiro	則	廣		Tamba	1684	5
Norikuni	則	國		Yamashiro	1222	180
Norikuni	則	國		Yamashiro	1661	5

Name of Smith				Province	Year	Value
Norimune	則	宗		Bizen	1184	210
Norimitsu	則	光		Bizen	1312	50
Norimitsu	則	光		Bizen	1394	15
Norimitsu	法	光		Bizen	1394	15
Norinaga	則	長	3?	Yamato	1320?	85
Norinari	則	成		Yamato	1312	90
Norisada	則	定		Yamashiro	1684	5
Norisada	則	定		Chikuzen	Present	5
Norishige	則	重		Etchû	1324	150
Norisue	則	末		Higo	1345	30
Noritaka	則	高		Bitchû	1184	145
Noritoshi	則	利		Etchû	1673	5
Noritsugu	則	次		Bizen	1210	150
Norizane	則	實		Bitchû	1190	150
Okihisa	興	久		Musashi	1615	15
Okimasa	興	正		Musashi	1681	45
Okinao	興	直		Musashi	1673	15
Rikiô	力	王		Yamato	1200?	100
Ryôkai	了	戒		Yamashiro	1288	110
Sa (Monji)	左			Chikuzen	1335	150
Sairen	西	蓮		Chikuzen	1307	140
Sadahide Jôshû	} 定	秀		Bungo	1160?	205
Sadahide	貞	秀		Musashi	1830	5
Sadahide	貞	秀		Settsu	1865	5
Sadahiro	貞	弘		Chikuzen	1381	15
Sadahiro	定	廣		Owari	1716	5
Sadakane	貞	包		Tamba	Present	5
Sadakatsu	貞	勝		Settsu	Present	5
Sadakazu	貞	一		Settsu	1834–1918	15
Sadakiyo	貞	清		Ôsumi	1317	35
Sadakiyo	貞	清		Yamato	1323	90

Name of Smith				Province	Year	Value
Sadakiyo	貞	清		Musashi	1684	5
Sadakuni	貞	國		Etchû	1362?	100
Sadakuni	貞	國		Echizen	1624	15
Sadamitsu	貞	光		Yamashiro	1365	85
Sadamune	貞	宗		Yamato	1318	145
Sadamune	貞	宗		Sagami	1331	160
Sadanori	定	則		Bizen	1144	150
Sadanori	貞	則		Settsu	1673	10
Sadaoki	貞	興		Yamato	1364	60
Sadashige	定	重		Mino	1661	5
Sadasuke	定	助		Bizen	1184	140
Sadatoshi	定	俊	2?	Yamashiro	1264	145
Sadatoshi	貞	俊		Rikuzen	1865	5
Sadatsugu	貞	次	4	Bitchû	1207	170
Sadatsugu	定	次		Yamashiro	1342	35
Sadatsugu	貞	次		Settsu	1661	5
Sadatsugu	貞	次		Iyo	Present	10
Sadatsuna	貞	綱		Iwami	1346	35
Sadayoshi	貞	吉		Yamato	1317	125
Sadayoshi	貞	吉		Chikuzen	1363	100
Sadayoshi	貞	吉		Settsu	1865	5
Sadayoshi	貞	吉		Echigo	Present	5
Sadayuki	貞	行		Chikuzen	1361	50
Sadayuki	貞	行		Bungo	1661	5
Sadayuki	貞	行		Musashi	1684	5
Sanea	實	阿		Chikuzen	1328	90
Sanefusa	眞	房		Bizen	1220	150
Sanefusa	眞	房		Bizen	1319	50
Sanekage	眞	景		Kaga	1368	95
Sanekage	眞	景		Bizen	1384	25
Sanekiyo	眞	清		Yamashiro	1100?	80
Sanemasa	實	昌		Hyûga	1368	25

Name of Smith				Province	Year	Value
Sanemitsu	眞	光		Bizen	1250 ?	100
Sanemori	眞	守		Hôki	950 ?	205
Sanemori	眞	守		Bizen	1288	50
Sanemoto	眞	元		Noto	1368	15
Sanenaga	眞	長	2	Bizen	1273	140
Sanenari	實	成		Bizen	1050 ?	195
Sanenori	眞	則		Izumo	1222	45
Saneo	眞	雄		Shinano	1818	10
Sanesada	眞	貞		Bizen	1256 ?	95
Sanetada	實	忠		Bizen	1394	15
Sanetoshi	眞	利		Yamashiro	1004 ?	170
Sanetoshi	眞	利		Bitchû	1234	125
Sanetsugu	眞	次		Bitchû	1220	125
Sanetsugu	實	次		Kii	1368	70
Sanetsuna	眞	繩		Hôki	980 ?	140
Sanetsuna	眞	綱		Iwami	1394	15
Sanetsune	實	經		Bizen	1220	150
Saneyuki	眞	行		Bitchû	1368	45
Saneyuki	實	行		Bungo	1673	5
Shigehiro	重	弘		Yamato	1207	160
Shigehisa	重	久		Yamato	1278	60
Shigeie	重	家		Bizen	1368	15
Shigekane	重	包		Chikuzen	1716	10
Shigekuni	重	國		Yamashiro	1375	25
Shigekuni	重	國		Kii	1615	35
Shigekuni	重	國		Kii	1673	10
Shigemasa	盛	昌		Musashi	1615	15
Shigemasa	鎭	政		Bungo	1624	5
Shigemasa	鎭	政		Iga	1624	5
Shigemitsu	重	光		Yamato	1200 ?	50
Shigemitsu	重	光		Yamashiro	1352 ?	85
Shigemitsu	重	光		Bizen	1362	90

Name of Smith			Province	Year	Value
Shigemistu	繁	光	Chikuzen	Present	5
Shigetoshi	繁	壽	Suruga	1870	5
Shigetsugu	重	次	Yamashiro	1394	15
Shigetsugu	重	次	Yamashiro	1596	5
Shigetsugu	繁	繼	Musashi	Present	5
Shigeyoshi	重	義	Yamashiro	1624	15
Shigeyuki	重	行	Bungo	1673	5
Shigeyuki	重	行	Uzen	1789	5
Shigezane	重	眞	Bizen	1335	95
Shimosaka	下	坂	Echizen	1688	5
Shinkai	眞	改	Settsu	1673	45
Shinryô	眞	了	Settsu	1661	10
Sueyuki	末	行	Bitchû	1225?	85
Sukechika	助	近	Bizen	1238	130
Sukefusa	助	房	Bizen	1213	140
Sukehide	助	秀	Bizen	1050?	150
Sukehira	助	平	Bizen	1081	205
Sukehira	祐	平	Bizen	1804	5
Sukehiro	助	廣	Sagami	1317	50
Sukehiro	助	廣	Settsu	1624	30
Sukehiro	助	廣	Settsu	1673	45
Sukekado	右	門	Suô	1844	5
Sukekane	助	包	Settsu	1661	5
Sukekuni	助	國	Bizen	1322	110
Sukekuni	祐	國	Settsu	1661	5
Sukemasa	助	政	Hidachi	1830	5
Sukemasa	助	政	Awa	1684	5
Sukemitsu	祐	光	Bizen	1469	25
Sukemori	助	茂	Bizen	1330?	100
Sukemune	助	宗	Bizen	1199	170
Sukemune	助	宗	Echizen	1624	5
Sukemune	助	宗	Suruga	1673	5

NAME OF SMITH				PROVINCE	YEAR	VALUE
Sukenaga	祐	永		Bizen	1830	5
Sukenao	助	直		Settsu	1688	35
Sukenao	助	直		Tosa	1848	5
Sukenobu	助	延		Bizen	1211	150
Sukenobu	助	信		Awa	1661	5
Sukenobu	助	信		Settsu	1673	5
Sukenori	則	則		Bizen	1213	150
Sukesada	祐	定		Bizen	1492	15
Sukesada Yosôzaemon	祐	定		Bizen	1504	35
Sukesada Hichibei no Jô	祐	定		Bizen	1624	10
Sukesada Ueno Daijô	祐	定		Bizen	1661	10
Sukeshige	助	重		Settsu	1673	15
Suketaka	助	高		Settsu	1688	10
Suketaka	助	隆		Settsu	1789	10
Suketomo	助	共		Hidachi	1861	5
Suketoshi	資	利		Izumi	1394	15
Suketsugu	助	次	2	Bitchû	1219	115
Suketsugu	助	次		Bizen	1330?	100
Suketsuna	助	綱		Sagami	1322	130
Sukeyoshi	助	吉		Bizen	1227	150
Sukeyoshi	祐	慶		Sagami	1304?	130
Sukeyoshi	助	義		Bizen	1330	115
Sukezane	助	眞		Sagami	1249?	170
Tadahiro II	忠	廣		Hizen	1648	10
Tadahiro IV	忠	廣		Hizen	1741	5
Tadakiyo	忠	清		Hizen	1661	5
Tadakuni	忠	國		Hizen	1624	10
Tadakuni	忠	國		Yamashiro	1624	5
Tadakuni	忠	國		Hizen	1684	5

Name of Smith			Province	Year	Value
Tadakuni	忠	國	Hizen	1688	5
Tadasada	忠	貞	Izumo	1394	15
Tadashige	忠	重	Settsu	1661	5
Tadashige	忠	重	Satsuma	1688	10
Tadatsuna	忠	綱	Settsu	1624	10
Tadatsuna	忠	綱	Settsu	1688	15
Tadatsuna Ômi no Kami III	忠	綱	Settsu	1716	5
Tadayori	忠	依	Mino	1220	30
Tadayoshi I	忠	吉	Hizen	1624	50
Tadayoshi Mutsu III	忠	吉	Hizen	1661	30
Tadayoshi Ômi no Daijô IV	忠	吉	Hizen	1688	5
Tadayoshi	忠	吉	Hizen	1748	5
Tadayuki	忠	行	Settsu	1661	5
Tadayuki	忠	行	Settsu	1688	5
Takahira	高	平	Bizen	1081 ?	205
Takahira	高	平	Kaga	1596	10
Takahisa	高	久	Echizen	1661	5
Takakane	高	包	Bizen	1099	190
Takamichi	貴	道	Owari	1624	5
Takemitsu	武	光	Higo	Present	5
Tamehiro	爲	廣	Settsu	1661	5
Tamekiyo	爲	清	2 ? Bizen	1099	115
Tametô	爲	遠	Bitchû	1150 ?	170
Tametsugu	爲	次	Bitchû	1211	100
Tametsugu	爲	繼	Etchû	1356	85
Tametsugu	爲	繼	Mino	1356	85
Tameyasu	爲	康	Kii	1624	10
Tameyoshi	爲	吉	Hôki	950 ?	170
Terufusa	昭	房	Awa	Present	5

NAME OF SMITH			PROVINCE	YEAR	VALUE
Teruhide	照	秀	Musashi	1818	5
Teruhiro	輝	廣	Aki	1596	10
Teruhiro	輝	廣	Aki	1661	5
Teruhiro	輝	廣	Aki	1673	5
Terukane	照	包	Settsu	1661	15
Terumasa	輝	政	Iyo	1661	5
Terumori	昭	盛	Shimotsuke	Present	5
Terutomo	昭	友	Musashi	Present	5
Tôfuchi	外	藤	Mino	1334	145
Tôchika	遠	近	Bizen	1160?	150
Tokinaka	辰	仲	Chikuzen	1688	5
Tokukatsu	德	勝	Hidachi	1865	5
Tokurin	德	隣	Hidachi	1804	10
Tomohide	友	秀	Musashi	1624	5
Tomokiyo	友	清	Yamato	1319	125
Tomokuni	倫	國	Yamashiro	1312	90
Tomomitsu	友	光	Bizen	1345	40
Tomomitsu	友	光	Yamato	1350?	190
Tomonari	友	成	Bizen	1100?	270
Tomotada Asatada	} 朝	忠	Mimasaku	1184	150
Tomoyasu	友	安	Bizen	1100?	170
Tomoyuki	友	行	Yamato	1368	30
Tomoyuki	友	行	Bizen	1661	5
Toshimasa	壽	正	Shinano	1830	5
Toshimune	俊	宗	Bizen	1312	35
Toshinaga	俊	長	Ômi	1360	100
Toshinaga	歳	長	Yamashiro	1661	10
Toshinaga	壽	命	Mino	1661	5
Toshisane	壽	實	Inaba	1818	5
Toshishige	利	重	Iwashiro	1661	5
Toshitsugu	俊	次	Bitchû	1211	115

Name of Smith				Province	Year	Value
Tsuguhide	次	英		Bitchû	1268	100
Tsuguhira	繼	平		Musashi	1661	10
Tsuguhiro	次	弘		Bitchû	1368	50
Tsuguhiro	繼	廣		Echizen	1661	5
Tsuguie	次	家		Bitchû	1207	150
Tsugunao	次	直	2	Bitchû	1268	100
Tsuguyori	次	依		Bitchû	1298	130
Tsuguyoshi	次	吉	3	Bitchû	1238	140
Tsuguyoshi	次	吉		Echigo	1384	25
Tsunahiro	綱	廣		Sagami	1658	10
Tsunahiro	綱	廣		Sagami	1818	5
Tsunaie	綱	家		Sagami	1504	15
Tsunamune	綱	宗		Rikuzen	1661	15
Tsunanobu	綱	信		Uzen	1830	5
Tsunatoshi	綱	俊		Uzen	1830	10
Tsunemitsu	常	光		Musashi	1624	10
Tsunetô	經	遠		Bizen	1150 ?	160
Tsunetô	常	遠		Bitchû	1184 ?	130
Tsunetsugu	恒	次	3	Bitchû	1207	170
Tsuyoshi	果			Ugo	Present	5
Ujifusa	氏	房		Owari	1555	13
Ujifusa	氏	房		Owari	1661	10
Ujinobu	氏	信		Mino	1681	5
Ujishige	氏	重		Satsuma	1661	5
Ujiyoshi	氏	吉		Awa	1379	15
Ujiyoshi	氏	善		Mino	1658	5
Ujiyoshi	氏	吉		Awa	1830	5
Undô	雲	同		Bizen	1334	95
Unji	雲	次	3	Bizen	1317	130
Unjô	雲	生	2	Bizen	1303	130
Unjû	雲	重		Bizen	1357	85
Yasuharu	康	春		Sagami	1521	15

NAME OF SMITH			PROVINCE	YEAR	VALUE
Yasuhiro	康	廣	Settsu	1661	10
Yasuhisa	安	久	Satsuma	1368	30
Yasuie	家	家	Bitchû	1312	130
Yasukuni	康	國	Sagami	1504	15
Yasukuni	安	國	Musashi	1711	10
Yasumasa	安	正	Satsuma	1688	5
Yasumitsu	安	光	Bizen	1390	15
Yasumitsu	康	光	Bizen	1394	60
Yasunaga	康	永	Bizen	1394	25
Yasunaga	康	永	Echizen	1673	5
Yasunobu	安	信	Echigo	1324 ?	70
Yasunori	安	則	Yamato	1000 ?	190
Yasunori	安	則	Bizen	1190	160
Yasunori	安	則	Satsuma	1352	55
Yasunori	安	代	Satsuma	1716	35
Yasusada	安	定	Musashi	1661	10
Yasutomo	安	倫	Mutsu	1661	10
Yasutoshi	安	俊	Satsuma	1345	60
Yasutsugu	安	次	Bitchû	1130 ?	160
Yasutsugu	康	次	Bitchû	1200 ?	140
Yasutsugu	安	次	Satsuma	1596	5
Yasutsugu	康	繼	Musashi	1624	15
Yasutsugu	康	繼	Musashi	1661	10
Yasutsuna	安	綱	Hôki	900 ?	270
Yasutsuna	康	綱	Hyûga	1394	10
Yasutsuna	安	綱	Kii	1661	5
Yasutsune	安	恒	Bitchû	1312	50
Yasutsune	安	常	Satsuma	1764	5
Yasuyoshi Sa	} 安	吉	Chikuzen	1335	150
Yasuyoshi	安	吉	Nagato	1363	115
Yasuyoshi	安	吉	Chikuzen	1624	5

Name of Smith				Province	Year	Value
Yasuyuki	安	行		Satsuma	1329	70
Yasuyuki	安	行		Satsuma	1661	10
Yasuyuki	安	行		Satsuma	1789	5
Yoritsuna	賴	綱		Iwami	1362	35
Yoriyasu	賴	安		Mutsu	1352	25
Yoshiaki	吉	明		Settsu	1868	5
Yoshifusa	吉	房	3	Bizen	1213	170
Yoshihira	義	平		Yamashiro	1704	30
Yoshihiro	義	弘		Etchû	1334	250
Yoshihiro	義	弘		Yamato	1353	100
Yoshihiro	吉	廣		Sagami	1362	35
Yoshihiro	吉	廣		Hizen	1648	5
Yoshihiro	吉	廣		Hizen	1661	5
Yoshihiro	義	廣		Rikuchû	1789	5
Yoshihiro	義	弘		Musashi	1818	5
Yoshiie	吉	家		Yamashiro	1004?	170
Yoshiie	吉	家		Hizen	1624	5
Yoshikado	吉	門		Mino	1624	5
Yoshikage	吉	景		Bizen	1338	25
Yoshikage	義	景		Bizen	1342	105
Yoshikane	義	兼		Bizen	1317	60
Yoshikane	吉	包		Ômi	1362	35
Yoshikane	吉	包		Chikuzen	1661	10
Yoshikuni	義	國		Yamashiro	1624	5
Yoshikuni	義	國		Hizen	1652	5
Yoshikuni	吉	國		Chikuzen	1661	5
Yoshimasa	吉	正		Inaba	1300?	140
Yoshimasa	賀	正		Izumi	1362	15
Yoshimasa	吉	政		Chikuzen	1661	5
Yoshimasa	吉	正		Echigo	1716	5
Yoshimichi	吉	道		Yamashiro	1624	10
Yoshimichi	吉	道		Settsu	1658	5

Name of Smith				Province	Year	Value
Yoshimichi	吉	道		Settsu	1661	10
Yoshimichi II Tamba	}吉	道		Settsu	1673	5
Yoshimichi	義	道		Yamashiro	1688	5
Yoshimitsu	吉	光		Yamashiro	1264	205
Yoshimitsu	義	光		Bizen	1321	85
Yoshimitsu	吉	光		Tosa	1338	50
Yoshimitsu	賀	光		Bizen	1394	15
Yoshimochi	吉	用		Bizen	1243	140
Yoshinaga	吉	長		Yamashiro	1260	45
Yoshinaga	吉	長		Hizen	1596	10
Yoshinao	能	直		Bungo	1368	15
Yoshinao	吉	直		Buzen	1444	15
Yoshinobu	吉	信		Yamashiro	1624	15
Yoshinobu	吉	信		Yamashiro	1624	5
Yoshinori	吉	則		Bizen	1362	25
Yoshinori	吉	則	3 ?	Yamashiro	1396	80
Yoshisada	吉	貞		Chikuzen	1346	100
Yoshisada	能	貞		Chikuzen	1368	25
Yoshisada	能	定		Bungo	1368	25
Yoshisada	吉	貞		Hizen	1624	5
Yoshisuke	義	助		Suruga	1661	5
Yoshitada	義	忠		Yamato	1698	5
Yoshitake	吉	武		Musashi	1688	10
Yoshitô	慶	任		Yamashiro	1844	5
Yoshitoshi	寶	壽		Uzen	1804	5
Yoshitsugu	吉	次	4 ?	Bitchû	1249	125
Yoshitsugu	吉	次		Yamashiro	1368	45
Yoshitsuna	吉	綱		Bizen	1362	30
Yoshiyuki	吉	行		Bungo	1661	5
Yoshiyuki	吉	行		Bungo	1661	5
Yukihide	行	秀		Bizen	1184 ?	140

Name of Smith				Province	Year	Value
Yukihira	行	平		Yamato	1174?	190
Yukihira	行	平		Bungo	1200?	190
Yukihira	行	平		Bungo	1688	5
Yukihiro	行	廣		Higo	1661	10
Yukihiro	行	廣		Hizen	1661	5
Yukikage	行	景		Inaba	1560	60
Yukikuni	行	國		Bizen	1207	150
Yukimitsu	行	光	2	Sagami	1304	150
Yukimitsu	行	光		Kaga	1345	15
Yukimitsu	幸	光		Bizen	1394	15
Yukimitsu	行	光		Kaga	1661	5
Yukinaga	行	長		Bungo	1624	5
Yukinobu	行	信		Yamato	1150?	130
Yukitsugu	幸	次		Bitchû	1362	45
Yukiyasu	行	安		Satsuma	1278	170
Yukiyoshi	行	吉		Bingo	1356	45

Bibliography

T HERE WERE well over five hundred books on swords, mountings, and smiths, in Japanese (some date from 1312) before the Meiji Restoration. However, none of these volumes may be relied upon solely, for errors crept into even the most careful studies.

There have been many intensive and complete books on the subject in recent years. However, not many of these books are available in English. The following is a list of the more outstanding publications:

BOOKS AND ARTICLES IN ENGLISH

The Complete Manual of the Old Sword (Translation: Author unknown) Tokyo: 1793. Swordmaking and swordsmiths; classification and descriptions of swords.

DOBREE, ALFRED. "Japanese Sword Blades," *Archaeological Journal.* 1905, Vol. 62 (Series 2, Vol. 12), pp. 1–18; 218–255.

FURNAS, WENDELL J. "Fortunes in Souvenir Swords," *Esquire* (Nov. 1946), Vol. XXVI, No. 5, p. 94.

GILBERTSON, EDWARD. "Japanese Sword Blades," *Transactions and Proceedings of the Japan Society*. London: 1898. IV, 186–214. Illustrated.

GUNSAULUS, HELEN C. *The Japanese Sword and its Decoration*. Chicago: Field Museum of Natural History, 1924. Anthropology Leaflet No. 20. 21 pp., 4 plates.

HAWLEY W. M. (Compiler.) Hollywood, California: 1945. No. 11 of the Oriental Culture Chart Series. Types, nomenclature, and general description of forging processes, care, history, smiths, etc.

HOMMA, JUNJI. *Japanese Sword* (Japanese Art Series). Tokyo: The National Museum, 1948. 72 pp., 10 plates. Nomenclature, general description of forging processes, care, history, smiths, etc.

INAMI, HAKUSUI. *Nippon-tô, The Japanese Sword*. Tokyo: Cosmo Publishing Co., 1948. 222 pp. General study of swords.

JOLY, HENRI L.; and INADA, HAGITARÔ. *Sword and Samé*. London: privately printed, 1913. 11 plates. Translation of Arai Hakuseki's "The Sword Book," in *Honchô Gunkikô*, and *The Book of Samé (Ko Hi Sei Gi)*, by Inaba Tsurio.

LYMAN, BENJAMIN SMITH. "Japanese Swords," Reprint: *Proceedings of the Numismatic Antiquarian Society, Philadelphia, 1890–91*. Philadelphia: 1892. 38 pp., 18 figs.

———. "Japanese Swords," *Journal of the Franklin Institute*, Philadelphia: 1895. 141 pp. 13 figs.

———. "Metallurgical and Other Features of Japanese Swords," *Journal of the Franklin Institute*. Philadelphia: 1896. 14 pp., 9 figs. Abstract of a lecture delivered before the Franklin Institute, November 8, 1895.

McClatchie, Thomas R. H. "The Sword of Japan: Its History and Traditions," *Transactions of the Asiatic Society of Japan (1874–1882)*. II, 50–56.

Mumford, Ethel Watts. "The Japanese Book of the Ancient Sword," *Journal of the American Oriental Society, 1905–6*. Vol. 26, pt. 2, pp. 334–410.

Robinson, B. W. *A Primer of Japanese Sword-Blades*. London: Victoria & Albert Museum, 1956. 94 pp. Basic study of sword blades.

Books in Japanese

Fujishiro, Yoshio. *Nippon Tôko Jiten (Shintô Hen)*. Tokyo: 1939. 402 pp. Contains rubbings of tangs of swords from the Shintô period.

———. *Nippon Tôko Jiten (Kotô Hen)*. Tokyo: 1939. Contains rubbings of tangs from the Kotô period.

———. *Tôken Zuroku*. Tokyo: 1934. 492 pp. Contains pictures and rubbings of swords.

Homma, Junji. *Kotô Shintô*. Vol. VIII of *Nippon Rekishi* (Japanese History). Tokyo: Iwanami Publishing Co., 1934. 36 pp. Concise study of swords.

———. *Kôtoku no Zôgan-mei Shu-mei nado to Kare no Kanshiki*. Tokyo: 1955. 20 pp. A study of inscriptions of (Honnami) Kôtoku (mid-sixteenth century) and his talent for appraising swords.

———. *Mei-tô Zufu*. Tokyo: 1935. Contains pictures of famous swords of Japan.

———. (Compiler). *Kokuhô Tôken Zufu*. Tokyo: 1936–39. Contains photos of 163 famous Japanese national-treasure blades.

HOMMA, JUNJI; and SATŌ, KANICHI. *Kotetsu Taikan.* Tokyo: The Society for the Preservation of the Japanese Sword, 1955. 89 pp., 152 plates. A study of Nagasone Kotetsu, of the Shintô period.

――――. *Kunihiro Taikan.* Tokyo: The Society for the Preservation of the Japanese Sword, 1954. 53 pp., 106 plates. A thorough study of Horikawa Kunihiro, a master of the early Shintô period.

HONNAMI, KŌSON. *Nippon-tô.* Tokyo: 1923. Vol. 1, 270 pp.; Vol. 2, 1073 pp. (Revised edition: *Nippon-tô Taikan,* 1942.) General study and appraisal of swords.

HONNAMI, KŌSON; and MUROTSU, GEITARŌ. *Tôkô Sôran.* Tokyo: 1926. 778 pp. Index of smiths.

HONNAMI; HOMMA; IWASAKI; KANZU; OKONOGI; OGURA; TAWARA; and others. *Nippon-tô Kôza.* 25 volumes (de luxe edition, 16 volumes). Tokyo: Yûzankaku Publishing Co., 1935. Over 5000 pp. The most complete study of swords.

IMAMURA and BETCHAKU. *Kenwa-roku.* Tokyo: 1880. Vol. 1, 331 pp.; Vol. 2, 314 pp. General study of swords.

ISHIWATARI, SHINTARŌ. *Shin-ô Tôken Zuihitsu.* Kamakura: 1956. 124 pp. Contains personal views and experiences with swords.

KAWAGUCHI, NOBORU. *Nippon-tô, Sono Rekishi.* Tokyo: Asahi News Company, 1956. No. 34 of the Asahi photo series. 64 pp. Photos and history of swords.

KAWAGUCHI, NOBORU. *Shintô Kotô Taikan.* Tokyo: Nanjin-sha Publishing Co., 1932. Vol. 1., 206 pp., 288 plates; Vol. II, 850 pp., 320 plates.

KAWAGUCHI; KOYABU; and KISHIMOTO. *Tôken Meijiten.* Tokyo: Nanjin-sha Publishing Co., 1928. 580 pp. Contains rubbings of tangs.

KOIZUMI, HISAO. *Nippon-tô no Kindai Kenkyû.* Tokyo: 1932, 302 pp. 192 plates. General study and pictures of swords.

Nihon Bijutsu Tôken Hozon Kyôkai (The Society for the Preservation of the Japanese Sword). *Oojyaku-sho.* Tokyo: 1955; Limited issue of one hundred copies. Reproduction of one of the oldest books on swords (c. 1500). Contains 860 rubbings of tangs of swords.

OMURA, KUNITARô. *Shumi no Tôken Renma-jutsu.* Tokyo: 1919. 92 pp. Contains information about polishing swords.

SATô, KANICHI. *Tôken Kantei Techô.* Tokyo: The Society for the Preservation of the Japanese Sword, 1955. 310 pp. Contains the nomenclature, general description of forging processes, care, smiths, schools, history, postwar history, etc., of the sword.

SHIMIZU, FUDOKU. *Nippon Tôken Hyôjun Kakaku.* Tokyo: Bijutsu Kurabu, 1939. 1144 pp. Index and price list of smiths.

SHIMIZU, TAKANORI. *Tôken no Shin-kenkyû.* Tokyo: 1929. 743 pp. General study of swords.

TAKASE, UKô (Compiler). *Shoka Hisetsu Kantô Shusei.* Tokyo: 1918. 443 pp. Collection of old books published in the Tokugawa period.

————. *Tôken Kantei Bikô.* Tokyo: 1918. 250 pp. General study of swords.

UCHIDA, SôTEN. *Dai Nippon Tôken Shinkô.* Osaka: 1933. 1000 pp. General study of swords.

UCHIDA, SÔTEN; and KASHIMA, ISAO. *Shintô Meisaku-shû.* Osaka: 1930. 209 pp., 192 plates. General study and pictures of swords of the Shintô period.

————. *Kotô Meisaku-shû.* Osaka: 1930. General study and pictures of swords of the Kotô period.

JAPANESE PERIODICALS

Kotô Shintô Kakaku-hyô. (Annual market-price listing of swords). Published by Hattori, Eiichi. 1, 8, Kyôbashi, Chûô-ku, Tokyo.

Tôken Bijutsu (Journal of Swords). Bi-monthly magazine of the Society for the Preservation of the Japanese Sword (Nihon Bijutsu Tôken Hozon Kyôkai, National Museum, Ueno, Tokyo). Averages 88 pp. Issue No. 49 published in January, 1958. A section in English is promised in the future.

Tôken to Rekishi (Sword and History). Bi-monthly magazine of the Tôken Hozon Kai, 1, 383 Daita, Setagaya-ku, Tokyo. Averages 50 pp. One of the oldest magazines in the field.

Glossary

ASHI—Various notches in tempered lines.
AYASUGI-HADA—Special type of curved grain.

BIZEN-ZORI—*See koshi-zori.*
BONJI—Sanskrit characters sometimes engraved on blades.
BÔSHI—Tempered lines on points. They are found in various styles.
BUKE—Members of the samurai class.
BUKE-ZUKURI—Mountings of the New Sword period. Worn inserted between the hip and the sash.

CHÔJI—"Clover-tree flower." Variety of tempered line characterized by a mushroom-shaped pattern.
CHOKUTÔ—A sword without curvature.
CHÛ-KISSAKI—A medium-sized point.
CHÛ-SUGUHA—A medium-width straight tempered line.

DAI-SHÔ—A pair of swords, one long and one short. Standard equipment for samurai of the New Sword period.
DAITÔ—A long sword. Its cutting-edge is over two *shaku* in length.
DÔRAN—Variety of tempered line characterized by a billowing pattern.

EBI-ZAYA—"Lobster scabbard." A type of scabbard with notches placed about an inch apart and having a full, broad tip, thought to resemble the tail of a lobster.

FUCHI—Pommel or metal sleeve on the hilt. *Fuchi* and *kashira* were usually paired and made by the same artist.

FUKA-KURI-JIRI—*See Taka-yamagata.*
FUKURA—Curvature of cutting-edge at the point.
FUKURA-KARERU—A straight-edge point.
FUKURA-TSUKU—A curved-edge point.
FUKURIN—*See Kin-fukurin.*
FUNA-GATA—A variety of tang shaped like a ship's bottom.
FURI-SODE—A variety of tang shaped like a kimono sleeve.

GIN—Silver.
GIN-GISE—Filled or veneered with silver. Commonly found on *habaki* and *seppa.*
GIN-SUJI—*See Kin-suji.*
GOMABASHI—A set of two thin grooves running parallel on the blade surface. *Hashi* means "chopstick."
GUNOME—Variety of tempered line characterized by a zigzag pattern.
GUNTO—Modern military swords.
GYAKU-TAKA-NO-HA—Inverted V-shaped file mark.
GYOBUTSU—The treasures of the imperial household. In olden times the treasures of the Ashikagas, the Toyotomis, and the Tokugawas were also classed as *gyobutsu.*
GYO-NO-MUNE—*See Ihori-mune.*

HA-AGARI KURI-JIRI—Uneven U-shaped tang-tip.
HABAKI—A collar inserted around a blade just below the guard. It assures a tight fit between the scabbard and blade.
HADA—Grain on the blade surface.
HA-GANE—Blade steel.
HAKO-MIDARE—Variety of tempered line characterized by a box-shaped pattern.
HA-MACHI—*See Machi.*
HARA-KIRI—Suicide by cutting one's abdomen.
HARI-MENUKI—A set of hilt ornaments attached without tapes or cords. Often found on ancient ceremonial *jin-dachi* as well as short swords of all ages. Also called *uki-menuki.*

HI—Grooves on the blade surface.

HIGAKI-YASURI—Checked file mark.

HIRA-MUNE—Flat ridge back.

HIRA-YAMAGATA—Double-beveled tang-tip. Also known as *kuri-jiri*.

HIRA-ZUKURI—Type of blade shape most commonly found in short swords.

HIRO-SUGUHA—A wide, straight tempered line.

HITATSURA—Irregular or full tempered line produced by many smiths of Sôshû.

HITSU—Handle section of a *kozuka*.

HO—Blade section of a *kozuka*.

HON-SANMAI-AWASE-GITAE—Type of blade construction characterized by a soft core, hard blade steel, and skin steel.

HOSO-SUGUHA—*See Ito-suguha.*

ICHI-MAI-BÔSHI—The area of a point which is completely tempered.

IHORI-MUNE—Inverted V-shaped ridge back. Also called *gyo-no-mune*.

IKARI-Ô-KISSAKI—A large curved point.

IKUBI-KISSAKI—A stout point with a straight cutting-edge. Often found on swords of the mid-Kamakura period.

INAZUMA—*See Kin-suji.*

ITAME-HADA—Wood grain.

ITO-SUGUHA—Narrow, straight tempered line. Also known as *hoso-suguha.*

JI—Blade surface.

JINDACHI—A blade in a *jindachi-zukuri* mounting. Sometimes simply called *tachi.*

JINDACHI-ZUKURI—Type of ancient mounting having two cords on the scabbard for suspension from the hip. The blade is usually over three *shaku*. Many ceremonial and decorative reproductions of this mounting were made after the *jindachi* became obsolete in the early sixteenth century.

JIZÔ-BÔSHI—Head-shaped tempered line on the point.

KAEN—Flame-shaped tempered line on the point.

KAERI—Turn back. Point at which the tempered line reverses.

KAERI-ASASHI—Short turn-back.

KAERI-FUKASHI—Long turn-back.

KAIGUNTÔ—Modern navy swords.

KAJI—Swordsmith. Also called *katana-kaji*.

KAKU-ICHI-MONJI—*See kiri*.

KAKU-MUNE—Flat ridge back. Also called *hira-mune*.

KANMURI-OTOSHI-ZUKURI—Variety of blade shape.

KANTEI—Appraising.

KANTEI-KA—An appraiser.

KASHIRA—Pommel at the base of the hilt. *See also fuchi*.

KATA-KIRI-BA-ZUKURI—A variety of blade shape.

KATANA—Sword. Sometimes refers only to long swords in distinction to short swords.

KATANA-MEI—The maker's signature on the *omote* of a tang. Except for the Tadayoshi School, of Hizen Province, almost all smiths of the New Sword period signed their names in this manner.

KATA-SHINOGI-ZUKURI—Variety of blade shape.

KATTE-SAGARI—Slightly slanted file marks.

KAWA-GANE—Skin steel.

KEN—Straight, double-edged sword with a ridge line down the center of the blade. *Ken* made in the New Sword period had *yokote*. Sometimes long blades of *yari* are converted into *ken* and mounted as swords.

KENGYÔ—V-shaped tang-tip.

KESHÔ-YASURI—Decorative "full-dress" file markings found on tangs of the New Sword period.

KE-ZAYA—Type of ancient scabbard. The end of the scabbard was wrapped with animal fur, such as that of the tiger or bear.

KIJI-MOMO NAKAGO—Variety of tang shaped somewhat like a pheasant thigh. Found only on swords made before the Kamakura period.

KIKU-ICHI-MONJI—Inscription of a chrysanthemum with the Chinese character for "one." Often found on tangs. Reputedly some of the old masters of Bizen Province who served under Emperor Gotoba were given the honor of using the imperial chrysanthemum crest in their inscriptions. Also, many smiths of the New Sword period used this crest.

KIKU-SUI—"Chrysanthemum and water." A tempered-line pattern found on swords of the New Sword period.

KIKU-NO-GYOSAKU—Swords supposedly forged by Emperor Gotoba. Instead of his signature, he inscribed chrysanthemum crests. The flowers were depicted as having sixteen, eighteen, or twenty-four petals.

KIN—Gold.

KIN-FUKURIN—Gold rim on guards or gold collar on scabbards of *tachi* mountings.

KIN-GISE—Veneered or filled with gold. Many mountings, such as *habaki* or *seppa*, were dressed in this manner with a thin layer of gold.

KIN-MEI—*Same as Kinpun-mei.*

KINPUN-MEI—"Gold-dust name." An appraiser's inscription in gold lacquer on a tang giving the name of the supposed swordmaker.

KIN-SUJI—A thin, radiant line of dark spots on the tempered-line area of the blade. It is similar to *suna-gashi* but is more radiant. *Gin-suji* is basically the same but is slightly duller in color. Zigzag *kin-suji* is called *inazuma* (lightning).

KIN-ZOGAN-MEI—An appraiser's inscription in gold inlay on a tang giving the name of the supposed maker.

KIRI—Horizontal file marks on a tang. Also known as *yoko* or *ichimon-ji*.

KIRI-HA-ZUKURI—A blade shape similar to *shinogi-zukuri* but with its *shinogi* line very close to the cutting edge.

KIRI-SUJI-CHIGAI—A type of combined horizontal and slanted file marks.

KISSAKI—Point section of a blade.

KITAE—Methods of combining blade steel.

KIZU—Blade defects caused at the time of forging or resulting from ill care.

Ko—Prefix meaning "small" or "old."

Ko-fuda—*See Sage-fuda.*

Ko-dachi—"Small *tachi.*" A forerunner of the *wakizashi.* This term refers to the mountings of small *tachi* used in the early and middle Kamakura periods.

Ko-dôgu—Sword furnitures, such as *kozuka, kôgai, tsuba, fuchi,* and *kashira.*

Kôgai—A skewer.

Koi-guchi—Opening of a scabbard.

Kojiri—End section of a scabbard.

Ko-kissaki—Small point of sword.

Ko-maru-bôshi—Tempered line on the point, small and circular in shape.

Konuka-hada—Extremely fine grain on blade surface. Often found on swords made by smiths of the Tadayoshi School, in Hizen Province. Also called *Hizen-hada.*

Koshi-ba—The area a few inches above the *ha-machi* with wider and wavier tempered lines than the rest of the blade. An almost exclusive feature of the swords of the Old Sword period.

Ko-shinogi—A section of the *shinogi* line above the *yokote.*

Koshirae—Sword mountings of olden times. Thus a *shira-saya* is not classed among *koshirae.*

Koshi-zori—Type of blade curvature. The deepest point of curvature appears much nearer the tang than the center of the blade. Often found in swords made by old Bizen smiths. Also called *Bizen-zori.*

Kosuji-chigai—*Same as Katte-sagari.*

Kozuka—Utility knife. Usually inserted in scabbard pocket. Consists of a *hitsu* (handle) and a *ho* (blade).

Kui-chigai—"Criss-crossed." A criss-crossed pattern of straight tempered lines or blade grooves.

Kuri-gata—Cord knob of scabbard.

Kuri-jiri—*See Hira-yamagata.*

Kurikara—Sanskrit: "black dragon." Engravings of *kurikara* are often found on blades.

KUWA-GATA—U-shaped metal piece attached to the base of the scabbard.

KYÛ-GUNTÔ—Proto-army swords.

MACHI—Small notches separating the tang from the blade. The notches on the cutting edge are called *ha-machi;* those on the back ridge are called *mune-machi.*

MAKURI-GITAE—A type of blade construction.

MARU-GITAE—A type of blade construction.

MARU-MUNE—Round ridge back. Also called *sô-no-mune.*

MASAME-HADA—Straight grain.

MEI—Signature of maker inscribed on sword.

MEKUGI—A peg, generally made of bamboo, used to fasten the blade into the hilt.

MEKUGI-ANA—Peg hole in the hilt.

MENUKI—Hilt ornaments.

MIDARE-KOMI-BÔSHI—Wavy tempered line on the point.

MIDARE-YAKI-BA—Wavy tempered line on the blade.

MIMI-GATA—Variety of tempered line characterized by an ear-shaped pattern.

MITOKORO-MONO—A set of *kozuka, kôgai,* and *menuki* by one maker.

MITSU-MUNE—Double ridge back. Frequently found on swords made by the Sôshû smiths. Also called *shin-no-mune.*

MOKUME-HADA—Burl grain.

MONO-UCHI—Striking area. Located approximately one-fourth of blade length from point.

MORO-HA-ZUKURI—A type of blade found on short swords.

MUJI—A type of blade construction. Also known as *muji tetsu.*

MUNE—Back or top ridge of blade.

MUNE-GANE—Steel used for the blade back.

MUNE-MACHI—*See Machi.*

MUNE-YAKI—Tempered line on top ridge of blade.

NAGAMAKI—Type of mounting for *naginata.*

NAGINATA—A kind of halberd. Blade is usually in the *unokubi-zukuri* style. Full length, including the handle and blade, is over six feet.

NAKAGO—The tang. The portion of the blade which is inserted in the handle.

NANBAN-TETSU—Imported steel.

NIE—*See Nioi.*

NIOI—Misty-white, fine martensite grain on the tempered area of a blade. A similar but coarser grain is called *nie.*

NISE—False or counterfeit.

NISE-MEI—Counterfeit signature of maker.

NOKOGIRI-BA—Tempered line characterized by a saw-tooth pattern.

NOTARE—Tempered line characterized by an undulating pattern.

Ô—Prefiix meaning "large."

O-KISSAKI—A large point.

Ô-MARU-BÔSHI—Large, circular tempered line on the point.

OMOTE—The side of the blade facing the holder when it is held upright with the cutting edge to the left. The reverse side is called the *ura.*

ORIGAMI—A certificate of appraisal.

OSHIGATA—A rubbing or impression of a tang or entire blade.

Ô-SURIAGE—*See Suriage.*

SAGE-FUDA—A small triangular certificate issued by the Honnami family in the Edo period for swords of lesser value. Also known as *ko-fuda.*

SAGEO—The cord which passes through the *kuri-gata.* It is usually made of silk. Its color ordinarily matches that of the hilt tape.

SAIDAN-MEI—Inscriptions, usually on the tang, giving the result of a cutting test.

SAI-HA—Retempering of a blade which has lost its original tempered line. Also called *sai-jin.*

SAI-JIN—*See Sai-ha.*

SAKA-ASHI—Oblique notched tempered line.

SAKI-ZORI—Blade curvature which is greatest at the *mono-uchi.*

SAME-GAWA—Skin of the giant ray. Used for binding handles and decorating scabbards.

S<small>AME-ZAYA</small>—Scabbard decorated with *same-gawa*.

S<small>AMURAI</small>—Warrior or knight of the feudal era.

S<small>ANBON-SUGI</small>—A set of three sharp pointed tempered lines characterized by a regular zigzag pattern. Almost exclusively a feature of the Kanemoto, or Magoroku, school of Seki Province.

S<small>ASHI-OMOTE</small>—*Same as omote.*

S<small>AYA</small>—Scabbard.

S<small>AYA-GAKI</small>—Identifying data about the maker of a blade written on the scabbard. Commonly found on *shira-saya*.

S<small>AYA-SHI</small>—A scabbard-maker.

S<small>ENSUKI</small>—Shaved marks on a tang.

S<small>EPPA</small>—Washer found between the collar and the guard. In swords of the *buke-zukuri* type it is also found between the guard and the hilt.

S<small>HIHO-ZUME-GITAE</small>—Type of blade construction.

S<small>HIMARU</small>—*See Urumu.*

S<small>HIN-GANE</small>—Core steel.

S<small>HIN-GUNTÔ</small>—Neo-army swords.

S<small>HIN-NO-MUNE</small>—*See Mitsu-mune.*

S<small>HINOGI</small>—Ridge line.

S<small>HINOGI-HIKUSHI</small>—Flat ridge line.

S<small>HINOGI-JI</small>—Upper blade surface. The area between the ridge line and the back ridge.

S<small>HINOGI-JI-SUJI-CHIGAI</small>—*Same as Kiri-suji-chigai.*

S<small>HINOGI-KIRI-SUJI-CHIGAI</small>—A type of combined horizontal and leftward-slanted file marks.

S<small>HINOGI-TAKASHI</small>—Raised ridge line.

S<small>HINOGI-ZUKURI</small>—A blade with ridge line.

S<small>HIN-SHINTÔ</small>—Swords made after 1868.

S<small>HINTÔ</small>—Swords made during the New Sword period.

S<small>HIRA-SAYA</small>—Plain wood scabbard.

S<small>HÔBU-ZUKURI</small>—A type of blade construction.

S<small>HÔWA-TÔ</small>—Swords made in the Shôwa era (since 1926).

S<small>O-NO-MUNE</small>—*See Maru-mune.*

S<small>ORI</small>—Blade curvature.

SORI-ASASHI—Shallow curvature.

SORI-FUKASHI—Deep curvature.

SUDARE-BA—Variety of tempered line characterized by a pattern reminiscent of a bamboo curtain *(sudare)*.

SUGUHA—Straight tempered line.

SUNA-GASHI—A formation of rough martensite sometimes found along tempered lines. It looks like a strip of scattered sand.

SURI-AGE—Sword with shortened tang. A sword shortened to the extent that it loses its original tang entirely is called *ô-suriage*.

TACHI—An ancient slung sword housed in a *jindachi* mounting.

TACHI-MEI—The signature of a sword's maker inscribed on the *ura* of the tang. Rarely was this done in the Shinto period, except by smiths of Hizen Province, such as those of the Tadayoshi School.

TAKA-NO-HA—Inverted V-shaped file mark.

TAKA-YAMAGATA—Sharp U-shaped tang-tip.

TANAGO-BARA—Variety of tang shaped somewhat like a fish's belly.

TANTÔ—A short sword. Less than one *shaku* in length.

TOBI-YAKI—Isolated tempered spots or islands on blade. Common on *hitatsura* blades.

TOGI—Sword polishing.

TORII-ZORI—A type of blade curvature. The deepest point appears at approximately the center of the blade.

TSUBA—A sword guard.

TSUKA—Hilt or handle.

TSUKA-ITO—Binding cord or tape on the *tsuka*.

TSUKURI—Old style mountings, exclusive of *shira-saya*.

TSUNAGI—Dummy blade of bamboo or wood. Used to keep furniture and mountings together in the absence of the original blade.

UBU-NAKAGO—An unshortened tang in its original form.

UCHI-GATANA—A sword in a *buke-zukuri* mounting. It was the longer of two swords commonly worn by samurai of the Edo period.

UCHI-KO—Finely powdered polishing stone used to remove old oil from a blade surface.

UDE-NUKI—A cord commonly passed through holes in the handle or guard of a *tachi* and tied to the wrist to prevent the sword from slipping from the hand.

UKI-MENUKI—*See Hari-menuki.*

URA—*See Omote.*

URA-MEI—Inscriptions on the *ura* of the tang. Commonly referred to as "date inscriptions." Most swords have their makers' names inscribed on the *omote.* and the date on the *ura.* Although the *tachi-mei* is on the *ura*, it is not classified as an *ura-mei.*

UNOKUBI-ZUKURI—A type of blade.

URUMU—A condition in which the blade edge is not sharp or the blade surface not clean. The opposite condition is called *shimaru.*

WAKIZASHI—A medium-sized blade over one *shaku* but less than two *shaku* in length.

WARIBA-GITAE—A type of blade construction.

WARI-BASHI—A set of split chopsticks similar in shape to a *kôgai.*

YAHAZU—Dovetail tempered line.

YAKI-BA—Tempered line.

YAKI-DASHI—The area a few inches above the *ha-machi* which has a straight or less-wavy tempered line than other areas. Only found on blades of the New Sword period.

YAKI-OTOSHI—Method of making a tempered line so that it starts an inch or so above the *ha-machi*, leaving a small portion of the blade without a tempered line. Used by a very small number of smiths in the Old Sword period.

YAKI-ZUME—A tempered line on the point without turn-back.

Old Provinces and Modern Prefectures

Alphabetical list of old provinces with corresponding modern equivalents. Numbers refer to map on page 20.

Aki (56), Hiroshima
Awa (16), Chiba
Awa (60), Tokushima
Awaji (47), Hyôgo
Bingo (54), Hiroshima
Bitchû (52), Okayama
Bizen (51), Okayama
Bungo (67), Ôita
Buzen (63), Fukuoka-Ôita
Chikugo (66), Fukuoka
Echigo (17), Niigata
Echizen (31), Fukui
Etchû (28), Toyama
Ezo (1), Hokkaidô
Harima (46), Hyôgo
Hida (27), Gifu
Higo (68), Kumamoto
Hitachi (10), Ibaraki
Hizen (65), Saga-Nagasaki
Hôki (49), Tottori
Hyûga (69), Miyazaki

Iga (34), Mie
Inaba (48), Tottori
Ise (35), Mie
Iwaki (8), Fukushima-Miyagi
Iwami (55), Shimane
Iwashiro (7), Fukushima
Iyo (61), Ehime
Izu (22), Shizuoka
Izumi (39), Osaka
Izumo (53), Shimane
Kaga (30), Ishikawa
Kai (20), Yamanashi
Kawachi (40), Osaka
Kazusa (15), Chiba
Kii (38), Wakayama-Mie
Kôzuke (11), Gumma
Mikawa (24), Aichi
Mimasaka (50), Okayama
Mino (26), Gifu
Musashi (12), Saitama-Tokyo-Kanagawa
Mutsu (2), Aomori-Iwate-Akita

Nagato (58), Yamaguchi
Noto (29), Ishikawa
Ômi (33), Shiga
Ôsumi (71), Kagoshima
Owari (25), Aichi
Rikuchû (4), Iwate
Rikuzen (6), Miyagi
Sado (18), Niigata
Sagami (14), Kanagawa
Sanuki (59), Kagawa
Satsuma (70), Kagoshima
Settsu (45), Hyôgo
Shima (36), Mie
Shimofusa (13), Chiba-Ibaraki
Shimozuke (9), Tochigi
Shinano (19), Nagano
Suô (57), Yamaguchi
Suruga (21), Shizuoka
Tajima (44), Hyôgo
Tanba (42), Kyoto

Tango (43), Kyoto
Tosa (62), Kôchi
Tôtômi (23), Shizu-
oka

Ugo (3), Akita-Ya-
magata
Uzen (5), Yamagata
Wakasa (32), Fukui

Yamashiro(41), Kyo-
to
Yamato (37), Nara

Alphabetical list of modern prefectures with corresponding old provinces.

Aichi: Mikawa-Owari
Akita: Ugo-Mutsu
Aomori: Mutsu
Chiba: Shimofusa-Kazusa-Awa
Ehime: Iyo
Fukui: Echizen-Wakasa
Fukuoka: Buzen-Chikuzen-Chikugo
Fukushima: Iwashiro-Iwaki
Gifu: Mino-Hida
Gumma: Kôzuke
Hiroshima: Aki-Bingo
Hokkaidô. Ezo
Hyôgo: Tajima-Harima-Awaji-Settsu
Ibaraki: Hitachi-Shimofusa
Ishikawa: Noto-Kaga

Iwate: Mutsu-Rikuchû
Kagawa: Sanuki
Kagoshima: Satsuma-Ôsumi
Kanagawa: Musashi-Sagami
Kôchi: Tosa
Kumamoto: Higo
Kyoto: Yamashiro-Tanba-Tango
Mie: Iga-Ise-Shima-Yamato-Kii
Miyagi: Rikuzen-Iwaki
Miyazaki: Hyûga
Nagano: Shinano
Nagasaki: Hizen
Nara: Yamato
Niigata: Echigo-Sado
Ôita: Buzen-Bungo

Okayama: Mimasaka-Bizen-Bitchû
Osaka: Izumi-Kawachi
Saga: Hizen
Saitama: Musashi
Shiga: Ômi
Shimane: Izumo-Iwami
Shizuoka: Suruga-Izu-Tôtômi
Tochigi: Shimozuke
Tokushima: Awa
Tokyo: Musashi
Tottori: Inaba-Hôki
Toyama: Etchû
Wakayama: Kii
Yamagata: Ugo-Uzen
Yamaguchi: Suô-Nagato
Yamanashi: Kai

Index